History Summarized

PERSIAN GULF, AFGHANISTAN, AND IRAQ WARS

WORLD
BOOK

www.worldbook.com

World Book, Inc.
180 North LaSalle Street
Suite 900
Chicago, Illinois 60601
USA

For information about other "History Summarized" titles, as well as other World Book print and digital publications, please go to **www.worldbook.com**.

For information about other World Book publications, call 1-800-WORLDBK (967-5325).

For information about sales to schools and libraries, call 1-800-975-3250 (United States) or 1-800-837-5365 (Canada).

Library of Congress Cataloging-in-Publication Data for this volume has been applied for.

History Summarized
ISBN: 978-0-7166-3800-1 (set, hc.)

Persian Gulf, Afghanistan, and Iraq Wars
978-0-7166-3805-6 (hc.)

Also available as:
ISBN: 978-0-7166-3815-5 (e-book)

Printed in China by Shenzhen Wing King Tong Paper Products Co., Ltd., Shenzhen, Guangdong
1st printing July 2018

STAFF

Writer: Tom Firme

Executive Committee

President
Jim O'Rourke

Vice President and
Editor in Chief
Paul A. Kobasa

Vice President, Finance
Donald D. Keller

Vice President, Marketing
Jean Lin

Vice President, International
Maksim Rutenberg

Vice President, Technology
Jason Dole

Director, Human Resources
Bev Ecker

Editorial

Director, New Print
Tom Evans

Manager
Jeff De La Rosa

Senior Editor
Shawn Brennan

Librarian
S. Thomas Richardson

Manager, Contracts and
Compliance
(Rights and Permissions)
Loranne K. Shields

Manager, Indexing Services
David Pofelski

Digital

Director, Digital Product
Development
Erika Meller

Digital Product Manager
Jonathan Wills

Manufacturing/Production

Manufacturing Manager
Anne Fritzinger

Production Specialist
Curley Hunter

Proofreader
Nathalie Strassheim

Graphics and Design

Senior Art Director
Tom Evans

Coordinator, Design
Development and Production
Brenda Tropinski

Senior Visual
Communications Designer
Melanie Bender

Senior Designer
Isaiah Sheppard

Media Editor
Rosalia Bledsoe

Senior Cartographer
John M. Rejba

TABLE OF CONTENTS

"History Summarized"

Each book in this series concisely surveys a major historical event or interrelated series of events or a major cultural, economic, political or social movement. Especially important and interesting aspects of the subject of each book are highlighted in feature sections. Use a "History Summarized" book as an introduction to its subject in preparation for deeper study or as a review of the subject to reinforce what has been studied about the topic.

What were the Persian Gulf, Afghanistan, and Iraq wars?

The Persian Gulf (1991), Afghanistan (2001-2014), and Iraq (2003-2011) wars were a series of post-Cold War (1945-1991) conflicts in the Middle East led by the United States. Each of the three wars came after the United States saw threats rising from Afghanistan and Iraq. In the Persian Gulf War, the United States sensed that peace was at risk when Iraq invaded neighboring Kuwait in 1990. The U.S. and allied forces attacked in 1991 to subdue Iraq's military and remove the Iraqi presence from Kuwait. Later in the 1990's, Iraqi leader Saddam Hussein flaunted his country's ability to develop destructive chemical weapons.

In the Afghanistan War, the United States determined that the Taliban, a militant Islamic group that controlled the country, had harbored terrorists responsible for the deadly Sept. 11, 2001 (also called 9/11), terrorist attacks in the United States.

U.S. President George W. Bush used the possibility of Hussein's deployment of weapons of mass destruction as the foundation of his case for the second Iraq war in 2003. Due to skepticism from some United Nations (UN) Security Council member nations, Bush did not build as broad of a coalition in the UN as the administration of his father, President George H. W. Bush, did for the Persian Gulf War. Still, major combat operations passed quickly as the United States and its allies forced the fall of the Iraqi government. The coalition scored additional wins with the deaths of Hussein, two of his sons, and other officials. However, the United States and its allies faced ongoing struggles in both Iraq and Afghanistan for years following major combat in the two countries.

Weeks of bombing by allied aircraft during the Persian Gulf War of 1991 left much of Baghdad, Iraq's capital, in ruins. Residents of the city lacked electric power and running water during most of the war.

CHAPTER ONE

Persian Gulf War of 1991

The Persian Gulf War of 1991 was fought in early 1991 between Iraq and a coalition of 39 countries organized mainly by the United States and the United Nations. The U.S. government called the war *Operation Desert Storm*. It took place chiefly in Iraq and the tiny oil-rich nation of Kuwait (*koo WYT* or *koo WAYT*). These two countries lie together at the northern end of the Persian Gulf.

The coalition had formed after Iraq invaded Kuwait on Aug. 2, 1990. After quickly gaining control of Kuwait, Iraq moved large numbers of troops to Kuwait's border with Saudi Arabia, triggering fears that Iraq would invade Saudi Arabia next. Iraq's actions were viewed with alarm by the world's industrialized countries, which relied on Kuwait and Saudi Arabia as primary sources of petroleum. Several coalition members sent troops to Saudi Arabia to protect it from possible attack.

On Jan. 17, 1991, after months of pressuring Iraq to leave Kuwait, the coalition began bombing Iraqi military and industrial targets. In late February, the coalition launched a massive ground attack into Kuwait and southern Iraq and quickly defeated the Iraqis. Coalition military operations ended on February 28.

The war resulted in immense human suffering in the Middle East and enormous material damage in Iraq and Kuwait. Hundreds of thousands of people were killed or wounded or became refugees. Economic measures taken against Iraq caused great hardship there. The war also caused severe environmental pollution in the region, as the Iraqis set hundreds of Kuwaiti oil wells on fire and dumped huge amounts of Kuwaiti oil into the Persian Gulf. In addition, the war triggered bloody revolts in Iraq by Kurds and Shī`ite (*SHEE eyet*) Muslim Arabs.

History of Iraq (pre-Persian Gulf War)

The world's first known civilization developed in Sumer (*SOO muhr*), now southeastern Iraq, about 3500 B.C. Sumer was part of Mesopotamia (*mehs uh puh TAY mee uh*), an area that included most of present-day Iraq and parts of Syria and Turkey. Other ancient civilizations, including Assyria (*uh SIHR ee uh*) and Babylonia (*BAB uh LOHN ee uh*), flourished along the Tigris (*TY grihs*) and Euphrates (*yoo FRAY teez*) rivers between about 3500 and 539 B.C.

In 539 B.C., the Persians conquered Mesopotamia. Greek and Macedonian armies under Alexander the Great took the area from the Persians in 331 B.C. Greek rule continued until the Parthians, from the Caspian Sea area, established control by 126 B.C. Except for brief periods of Roman rule, the Parthians controlled Mesopotamia until about A.D. 224. That year, the Persian Sasanian *dynasty* (family of rulers) overthrew the Parthian Empire. The Sasanians ruled for about 400 years.

Arabs conquered the Sasanians in 637. The Arabs brought the religion of Islam and the Arabic language to Mesopotamia. The Abbasid dynasty came to power in 750 and soon founded Baghdad as the capital of the Islamic Empire. Under the Abbasids, Arab civilization reached great heights. By 800, Baghdad had nearly a million people and was a world center of trade and culture.

In 1258, Mongols from central Asia invaded Mesopotamia and destroyed the Islamic Empire. The Mongols neglected Mesopotamia, and the region deteriorated culturally and economically under their rule.

The Ottoman Empire, based in what is now Turkey, began to control

In 1258, Mongols from central Asia invaded Mesopotamia and destroyed the Islamic Empire. This painting depicts Mongols attacking Baghdad that year.

Mesopotamia in the early 1500's. The Ottomans battled with the Persians and local Arab leaders to maintain control.

During the 1700's and 1800's, the Ottoman Empire declined in power and size in the face of new, strong nations that developed in Europe. The United Kingdom became involved in the Persian Gulf region in the 1800's to protect its trade routes with India, which was then under British rule. By World War I (1914-1918), the United Kingdom had become interested in Mesopotamia's oil resources.

British troops took over Mesopotamia during World War I. In 1920, the League of Nations, a forerunner to the United Nations, gave the British a *mandate* (order to rule) over the area. The British set up a new government there in 1921. They renamed the country Iraq and chose an Arab prince as King Faisal I (*FY suhl*).

During the 1920's, British advisers retained positions in the Iraqi government, and the British controlled Iraq's army, foreign policy, finances, and oil resources. Some Iraqis opposed British involvement, and a movement for independence developed.

Under pressure from Iraq's independence movement, the United Kingdom signed a treaty with Iraq in 1930. In the treaty, the British promised military protection and eventual independence for Iraq. In return, Iraq promised the United Kingdom continued use of British air bases in Iraq. It also agreed to use British foreign advisers only. The British mandate over Iraq ended in 1932, and Iraq joined the League of Nations as an independent country.

In the 1930's, Iraq's politicians disagreed over the alliance with the

The British set up a new government in Mesopotamia in 1921. They renamed the country Iraq and chose an Arab prince as King Faisal I (seated, front).

United Kingdom. King Faisal worked to balance the interests of Iraq's political factions and to unify the country's ethnic and religious groups. Faisal died in 1933, and his son Ghazi became king. Ghazi was a weak ruler, and tribal and ethnic rebellions broke out. In 1936, anti-British groups in the army took control of the government, though Ghazi officially was still king. Ghazi died in 1939. His 3-year-old son, Faisal II, became king, but the boy's uncle, Prince Abdul Ilah (*ahb DOOL EE lah*), ruled for him.

In 1940 and 1941, during World War II, Iraqi government leaders and army officers sought an alliance with the Axis powers of Germany, Italy, and Japan. They hoped the alliance would end British influence in Iraq. The British tried to use Iraq as a military base in the war, as authorized under the 1930 treaty, and an armed conflict broke out. The British defeated the Iraqi army in 1941, and the pro-Axis leaders left the country. Iraq declared war on the Axis in 1943.

Inflation and supply shortages brought on by World War II transformed Iraq's society and economy. A wide economic gap developed between the rich and poor. Many Iraqis blamed the government for their economic situation.

In 1948, Iraq joined other Arab countries in a war against the new nation of Israel. The Arab defeat in the war touched off protests in Iraq and other Arab lands.

In 1950 and 1952, Iraq signed new agreements with foreign oil companies. The 1952 deal gave Iraq half of the profits from oil drilled there. Because of the agreements, Iraq's oil revenues rose dramatically. The government used some of this money to build hospitals, irrigation projects, roads, and schools. But the increased amount of money also caused serious inflation.

King Faisal II took full power in 1953 at the age of 18. In the 1950's, opposition to the monarchy grew. Many Iraqis wanted a voice in government. Others felt that they had not benefited enough from Iraq's oil profits. In addition, many Iraqis opposed the government's ties to the West. They objected to the Baghdad Pact—a U.S.-supported mutual defense *accord* (agreement) that Iraq signed with Iran, Pakistan, Turkey, and the United Kingdom in 1955. Many Iraqis felt that the ties with the West went against the *Pan-Arabism* movement. Advocates of Pan-Arabism believed that Arab countries should strive for political unity and be free of outside influence. In 1958, army officers overthrew the government and declared Iraq a republic. The rebels killed King Faisal and Prince Abdul Ilah.

The army officers set up a three-man Sovereignty (*SOV ruhn tee*) Council consisting of a Shī`ite Arab, a Kurd, and a Sunni Arab. The council issued a temporary constitution, giving a cabinet the power to rule by decree with the council's approval. General Abdul Karim Kassem (*ab DOOL kah REEM KAW sehm*) (also spelled Qasim), who led the revolution, became Iraq's premier. He reversed Iraq's pro-West policy and accepted both economic and military aid from Communist countries. He worked to develop industry in Iraq and set up land reform programs intended to narrow the gap between rich and poor.

In 1961, Kurdish leaders asked Kassem to give the Kurds complete *autonomy* (self-rule) within Iraq and a share of the revenues from oil fields in northern Iraq. Kassem rejected the plan. In response, the Kurds revolted. A ceasefire was finally declared in 1964.

In 1963, army officers and supporters of the Pan-Arabism movement assassinated Kassem. The Pan-Arabists, led by the Baath Party, took control of Iraq. They named Abdul Salam Arif (*ab DOOL sah LAHM AH rihf*) president and Ahmad Hasan al-Bakr (*ah MAHD huh SUHN ahl BAH kuhr*) prime minister. Both were army officers. Later that year, Arif used

In 1958, army officers overthrew Iraq's government and declared Iraq a republic. The rebels killed King Faisal and Prince Abdul Ilah. General Abdul Karim Kassem (right), who led the revolution, became Iraq's premier. Colonel Abdul Salam Arif (left) became vice premier.

the military to take over the government and remove the Baath Party from power. Arif died in 1966, and his brother, Abdul Rahman Arif (*ab DOOL rah MAN AH rihf*), became president. Both Arifs followed socialist economic policies.

Bakr overthrew Arif in 1968 and reestablished Baath control. The Baath Party soon began to dominate all aspects of Iraqi politics. Party leaders wrote a new constitution in 1970 that institutionalized Baath control of the government. Bakr supported further socialist economic reform and stronger ties with the Soviet Union. During Bakr's presidency, Saddam Hussein (*sah DAHM hoo SAYN*), who held important party and government posts, gained influence.

In 1973, the Iraqi government completed a takeover of foreign oil companies in the country. This *nationalization* of the oil industry made Iraq instantly wealthy.

In 1970, Bakr signed an agreement with the Kurds that ended years of on-and-off fighting. The government promised that, beginning in 1974, the Kurds would have self-rule and several posts in the government. New fighting erupted in 1974 after the Kurds objected to revisions in the agreement. The revised agreement gave limited autonomy to the Kurds in the Kurdish Autonomous Region in northern Iraq. Government forces largely defeated the Kurds by March 1975. After Bakr resigned as president in 1979, Saddam Hussein succeeded him.

In September 1980, Iraq invaded Iran, and war broke out. The war resulted partly from boundary disputes, from Iran's support of the rebellious Kurds, and from the efforts of Shī`ite leaders in Iran to incite rebellion in Iraq's Shī`ite population. Also, Iraqi leaders believed Iran had become somewhat unstable as a result of its 1979 Islamic revolution. They felt Iran's weakened position offered Iraq a chance to build its power in the region.

The war lasted eight years. Over 150,000 Iraqi soldiers died. Iranian air attacks on major cities wounded and killed many Iraqi civilians. The war also severely damaged Iraq's economy. Bombs damaged oil facilities in southern Iraq, and Persian Gulf trade was disrupted. Iraq and Iran agreed on a ceasefire in August 1988.

In September 1980, Iraq invaded Iran, and war broke out. In this photograph, Iraqi soldiers come into conflict with Iranian troops along the border region of Iran and Iraq in July 1984. The war lasted eight years. Over 150,000 Iraqi soldiers died.

During the war with Iran, Iraq's Kurds supported Iran. In 1987 and 1988, the Iraqi government lashed out against the Kurds. The army released poison gas in Kurdish villages, killing thousands of people. There also were reports that the army destroyed several Kurdish towns and that the inhabitants fled to Turkey and Iran.

History of Kuwait (pre-Persian Gulf War)

Kuwait had few settled inhabitants before 1700. About 1710, some members of the Arab Anaza tribal confederation settled on the southern shore of Kuwait Bay, where they found fresh water. These people built a port that later became the city of Kuwait. Between 1756 and 1762, the group elected the head of the Al-Sabah family to rule them as Sabah I.

In 1775, the British made Kuwait the starting point of their desert mail service to Aleppo, Syria. This route formed part of a system that carried goods and messages from India to England. Over the years, British interest in Kuwait grew. In 1899, the United Kingdom became responsible for Kuwait's defense.

In 1934, Kuwait's ruler granted a *concession* to allow the Kuwait Oil Company, a joint American-British enterprise, to drill for oil. Drilling began in 1936. Surveys showed that vast quantities of petroleum lay under the desert. Kuwait became a major petroleum exporter after World War II ended in 1945. It soon changed from a poor land to a wealthy one because of profits from oil sales. Kuwait joined the Arab League after it became independent in 1961. It joined the United Nations in 1963.

Kuwait sent troops to Egypt during the Middle East crisis in June 1967. But these troops did not take part in the Arab-Israeli war. For about two months, Kuwait cut off its oil shipments to the United States and other Western countries. Kuwait also agreed to pay Egypt and Jordan a total

Saddam Hussein

Saddam Hussein (*sah DAHM hoo SAYN*) (1937-2006) was president of Iraq from 1979 to 2003. His rule ended shortly after United States and allied forces invaded Iraq in March 2003. This invasion marked the start of the Iraq War (2003-2011). United States troops captured Hussein in December 2003. He was executed by Iraqi authorities on Dec. 30, 2006.

Hussein ruled Iraq as a dictator and was known for his ruthless actions. For example, in the late 1980's, he authorized the relocation or extermination of hundreds of thousands of Kurdish people in northern Iraq. This campaign included the frequent use of chemical weapons against the Kurds.

In August 1990, Hussein ordered Iraqi forces to invade and occupy Kuwait. The United Nations (UN) Security Council authorized military action to expel the Iraqi troops from Kuwait. In January 1991, a coalition of nations, organized mainly by the United States and the UN, began an air war against Iraq. After more than five weeks of bombing, coalition ground troops entered Iraq and Kuwait and quickly defeated the Iraqi forces.

During the 1990's and early 2000's, Iraq continued to have tense relations with many countries, particularly the United States. In March 2003, forces led by the United States began a military campaign against Iraq. The following month, the U.S.-led forces seized control of Baghdad, Iraq's capital, causing the fall of Hussein's government. U.S. officials said the main reason for the war was to disarm Iraq of *weapons of mass destruction*—that is, chemical, biological, or nuclear weapons. However, in the months following the U.S.-led invasion, search teams found no such weapons in Iraq.

In July 2003, Hussein's sons Uday (*oo DAY*) and Qusay (*KOO say*), who had held high-ranking positions in their father's regime, were killed in a firefight with U.S. troops. On Dec. 13, 2003, U.S. troops captured Saddam Hussein after they found him hiding near his hometown of Tikrit (*tih KREET*). In 2005, an Iraqi court formally charged Hussein with ordering the massacre of over 140 Shi`ites in 1982. In 2006, the court charged him with genocide for killing over 100,000 Kurds in the 1980's. In November, the court convicted Hussein of the Shi`ite massacre charges and sentenced him to death by hanging. He was executed the following month.

Saddam Hussein al-Tikriti was born on April 28, 1937, near Tikrit. He joined the Baath Party in 1957. In 1959, Hussein took part in an attempt to kill Iraqi prime minister Abdul Karim Kassem (also spelled Qasim). After the attempt failed, Hussein fled to Syria and then to Egypt. There, he studied law at Cairo University. In 1963, Baath officers captured and killed Kassem, and Hussein returned to Iraq. But later in 1963, the Baath government was overthrown, and in 1964, Hussein was imprisoned. He escaped from jail in 1966.

The Baath Party regained control of Iraq in 1968, and Hussein quickly became one of the most powerful people in the Baath government. In 1969, he was vice chairman of the party's Revolutionary Command Council (RCC). In 1979, he became chairman of the RCC and president of Iraq. Iraq's development program was halted by a war between Iraq and Iran, which lasted from 1980 to 1988.

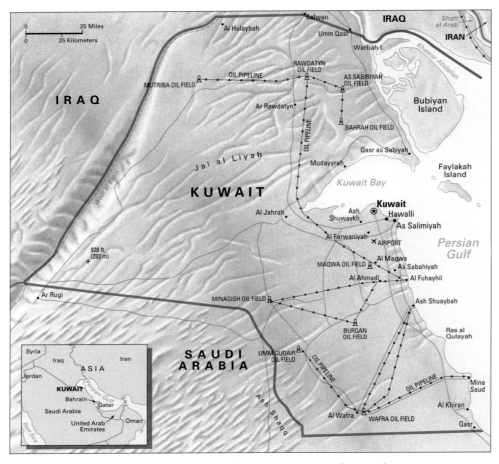

Kuwait is a small Arab country in southwestern Asia, at the north
end of the Persian Gulf. It is bordered by Iraq and Saudi Arabia.
This desert land is one of the world's leading petroleum producers.
It has almost one-tenth of the world's known reserves.

of $132 million annually to help their economies recover after the war.

A small number of Kuwaiti troops took part in the 1973 Arab-Israeli
War. In October 1973, Kuwait and other Arab oil-exporting nations
stopped shipments of oil to the United States and the Netherlands. They
also reduced shipments to other countries that supported Israel. In

March 1974, full shipments were renewed. In 1975, Kuwait's government *nationalized* (took control of) the Kuwait Oil Company. The government now has almost complete control of the oil industry.

In 1976, Kuwait's prime minister denounced the National Assembly for blocking legislation. Kuwait's emir, Sheik Sabah al-Salim al-Sabah, then dissolved the Assembly. In 1977, Sheik Sabah died, and his cousin Sheik Jabir al-Ahmad al-Jabir al-Sabah automatically succeeded him as emir. A new National Assembly was elected in 1981, but Sheik Jabir dissolved it and suspended the constitution in 1986.

In the 1980's, much fighting in a war between Iran and Iraq centered in the Persian Gulf area. In 1986, Iran began attacks on Kuwaiti oil tankers because of Kuwait's financial aid to, and other support for, Iraq.

Oil drilling began in Kuwait in 1936. Surveys showed that vast quantities of petroleum lay under the desert. In this photograph, pipes convey oil from Mina-al-Ahmadi harbor in Kuwait to an off-shore jetty in the 1930's.

In 1987, Kuwait asked the Soviet Union and the United States to help provide safety for its shipping. The Soviet Union leased to Kuwait vessels flying the Soviet flag. Several Kuwaiti ships were reregistered as U.S. vessels and flew U.S. flags. U.S. warships began escorting these vessels in the Persian Gulf to protect them from attacks. Some clashes between the U.S. forces and Iranians occurred. In August 1988, Iran and Iraq agreed to a cease-fire in their war.

Conditions for war

The Persian Gulf War of 1991 was the first major international crisis after the end of the Cold War (1945-1991). The crisis tested cooperation between the United States and the Soviet Union, as well as the ability of the UN to play a leading role in world affairs. The war also split the Arab world between coalition members and supporters of Iraq's president, Saddam Hussein.

Hussein's ambition for power and leadership in the Organization of the Petroleum Exporting Countries (OPEC) and in the Middle East was a central cause of the invasion of Kuwait. From 1980 to 1988, Iraq had fought a war with its neighbor Iran. Iraq suffered serious economic damage in the Iran-Iraq War. Nevertheless, it emerged from that war as the second-strongest military power in the Middle East. Only the Jewish state of Israel was stronger.

Hussein argued that Iraq had become the region's chief power opposed to Israel and should thus be recognized as leader of the Arab world. Since the late 1940's, Arab countries had fought several wars with Israel. Many Arabs wanted to abolish Israel and place its lands under the control of Palestinians and other Arabs.

Hussein claimed that, as leader of the Arab world, Iraq should receive help from other Arab countries in rebuilding its economy. According to

Hussein, Iraq needed help from OPEC in raising world oil prices, and Iraq needed Kuwait and other Arab countries to cancel debts that Iraq had incurred to fight the Iran-Iraq War.

After the Iran-Iraq War, Hussein had disagreed with Kuwait's leaders over how much debt cancellation and other aid Kuwait should provide to Iraq. Hussein also accused Kuwait of exceeding oil production limits set by OPEC and thus lowering world oil prices. In addition, Hussein claimed that Kuwait was taking Iraqi oil from the Rumaila (*roo MAY luh*) oil field, a large field that lay beneath both Iraq and Kuwait.

Also, Iraq had often claimed that Kuwait should be part of Iraq. Iraq based its claim on the fact that, in the late 1800's and early 1900's, Kuwait had been included in a province of the Ottoman Empire, called Basra, which later became part of Iraq. But by the time Iraq was formed in the early 1920's, Kuwait was no longer part of the province. Also by the early 1920's, the United Kingdom had gained control of Kuwait and what became Iraq. Iraq gained independence in 1932, and Kuwait in 1961. After 1961, disputes continued between Kuwait and Iraq over the location of their common border.

Several factors prompted Hussein to invade Kuwait. He wanted to acquire Kuwait's oil wealth and erase Iraq's debt to Kuwait. He wanted to increase Iraq's power within OPEC. He also sought better access to the Persian Gulf. Iraq's gulf coastline was short. Kuwait's was much longer and included an excellent harbor. In addition, Hussein probably hoped that an invasion would keep Iraq's military occupied and so end a series of attempts by the military to force him out of power.

An international crisis

At 2:00 a.m. on Aug. 2, 1990, hundreds of tanks and other Iraqi forces swept across the border into Kuwait. Within 24 hours, Iraq had com-

The Gulf Cooperation Council is a six-member organization of Arab states that works together in military defense and economic issues. Its members are Bahrain, Kuwait, Oman, Qatar, Saudi Arabia, and the United Arab Emirates. The council formed in 1981.

plete control of Kuwait. Thousands of Iraqi troops then moved to Kuwait's border with Saudi Arabia. To some, this movement signaled that Iraq might invade Saudi Arabia. On August 8, Iraq announced that it had annexed Kuwait.

Under international law, none of Iraq's claims against Kuwait justified the invasion. The United Nations, as well as the United States and many other countries, condemned the Iraqi invasion. But Hussein accused the United States of following a double standard. He said that if the United States condemned the Iraqi invasion, it should also condemn Israel's occupation of lands won from Arab countries in the Arab-Israeli wars. Since the 1970's, the United States had been Israel's chief ally.

Many Arabs, particularly poor Arabs and Palestinians, supported the Iraqi invasion. Hussein became a hero to them by confronting Israel and the United States. He gained additional support from poor Arabs by calling for the redistribution of the vast wealth of Kuwait, Saudi Arabia, and certain other Arab oil-exporting countries.

However, the Gulf Cooperation Council (a six-member organization of Arab states that works together in military defense and economic issues that includes Bahrain, Oman, Qatar, Saudi Arabia, Kuwait and the United Arab Emirates) condemned Iraq's invasion of Kuwait and demanded complete, unconditional withdrawal of Iraqi troops from Kuwait. Member countries of the council sided with the United States and its allies.

On August 2, the UN Security Council issued a resolution condemning Iraq's invasion. United States President George H. W. Bush and other world leaders began to form an anti-Iraq coalition. The coalition grew to include Afghanistan, Argentina, Australia, Bangladesh, Belgium, Canada, Czechoslovakia, Denmark, France, Germany, Greece, Honduras, Hungary, Italy, the Netherlands, New Zealand, Niger, Norway, Pakistan, Poland, Portugal, Senegal, Sierra Leone, Singapore, South Korea, Spain, Sweden, Turkey, the United Kingdom, and the United States. Arab members of the coalition were Bahrain, Egypt, Kuwait, Morocco, Oman, Qatar, Saudi Arabia, Syria, and the United Arab Emirates. The Arab countries of Jordan, Libya, and Yemen opposed the involvement of non-Arab countries but did not fight against the coalition. China and the Soviet Union, then the most powerful Communist countries, did not join the coalition. But their cooperation as members of the UN Security Council allowed the UN to play a leading role in the crisis.

On August 6, the UN Security Council imposed an embargo that prohibited all trade with Iraq except for medical supplies and food in certain circumstances. Nearly all of Iraq's major trading partners supported the embargo. As a result, Iraq's foreign trade was sharply reduced. On August 7, the United States announced that it would send troops to the Persian Gulf to defend Saudi Arabia from possible attack by Iraq.

On August 25, the UN Security Council authorized the use of force to carry out the embargo against Iraq. On November 29, the council gave coalition members permission "to use all necessary means" to expel Iraq from Kuwait if Iraq did not withdraw by Jan. 15, 1991. Iraq chose to stay in Kuwait.

By mid-January, the coalition had about 670,000 troops, 3,500 tanks,

General H. Norman Schwarzkopf

Herbert Norman Schwarzkopf, Jr., (1934-2012) was a general in the U.S. Army. He commanded the U.S. forces in the Persian Gulf War of 1991. Over 540,000 men and women served in the ground, sea, and air forces under his command.

Schwarzkopf was born on Aug. 22, 1934, in Trenton, New Jersey, the son of a major general in the U.S. Army. He graduated from the U.S. Military Academy at West Point in 1956. In 1964, he received a master's degree in mechanical engineering from the University of Southern California.

During the Vietnam War (1957-1975), Schwarzkopf served twice in Vietnam—in 1965 and 1966, and in 1969 and 1970. He then commanded troops in the United States and held staff positions in the Pentagon. During the U.S. military operation in Grenada in 1983, Schwarzkopf was deputy commander of the joint task force and principal Army adviser. In 1988, he was appointed commander in chief of U.S. Central Command, the headquarters for military operations in 18 countries of Africa and Asia.

Schwarzkopf retired from the Army in August 1991. In 1992, he wrote an autobiography, *It Doesn't Take a Hero.* He died on Dec. 27, 2012.

This map shows the locations in the Middle East where the Persian Gulf War of 1991 took place. The war began when a coalition of 39 countries invaded Iraq following that country's invasion of Kuwait. The United States and the United Nations were the main organizers of the coalition. The war was fought mainly by air and land forces in Iraq, Kuwait, and Saudi Arabia and by naval forces in the Persian Gulf. Iraq also launched missile attacks against Israel. Most ground fighting occurred in desert regions.

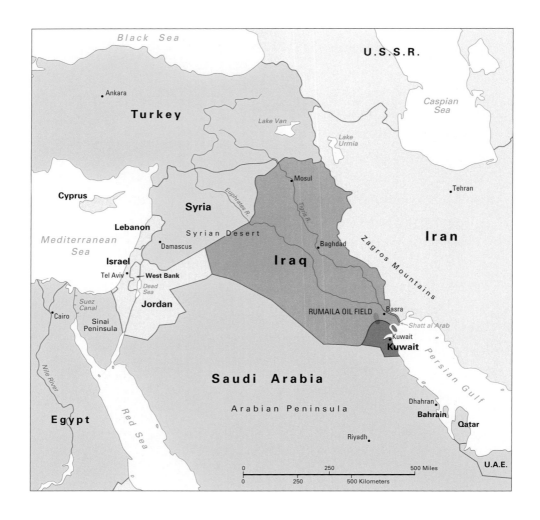

and 1,800 combat aircraft in the Persian Gulf region. The troops came from 28 coalition members and included about 425,000 troops from the United States. Many of the other troops came from the United Kingdom, France, and such Arab countries as Egypt, Saudi Arabia, and Syria. Other coalition members provided equipment, supplies, or financial aid. The coalition also had about 200 warships in the Persian Gulf region, including 6 U.S. aircraft carriers and 2 U.S. battleships. Iraq had between 350,000 and 550,000 troops in Kuwait and southern Iraq, with about 4,500 tanks and 550 combat aircraft. It also had a small navy.

Militarily, the coalition first tried to force Iraq to withdraw from Kuwait by bombing Iraqi military and industrial targets. But after more than five weeks of heavy bombing, Iraq still refused to withdraw. The allies then started a major ground attack against Iraqi forces.

U.S. General H. Norman Schwarzkopf commanded the U.S. forces in the Persian Gulf War of 1991. Over 540,000 men and women served in the ground, sea, and air forces under his command.

War begins

The air war began at 3 a.m. on Jan. 17, 1991. The coalition aimed first to destroy Iraq's ability to launch attacks. Other goals included eliminating Iraq's biological, chemical, and nuclear weapons facilities; disrupting its ability to gather information about coalition forces and to communicate with its own forces; and reducing the readiness of Iraqi troops.

Allied aircraft first bombed Baghdad, the capital of Iraq, and then attacked targets throughout Iraq and Kuwait. The allies gradually focused heavy bombing on Iraqi troops; artillery and tanks; transportation routes; and supplies of ammunition, food, fuel, and water.

The coalition achieved many of its objectives in the air war, in part because of the use of such high-technology equipment as night-vision systems and precision-guided weapons. These weapons included cruise missiles launched from U.S. ships in the gulf.

Before the war began, the coalition moved huge amounts of equipment to the Persian Gulf region in one of the largest airlifts in history. The United States Air Force used precision-guided "smart" bombs and the F-117 "stealth" fighter-bomber. The special design and surface materials of "stealth" bombers make them difficult to detect with radar. The coalition quickly gained control of the air, destroying many Iraqi aircraft on the ground and forcing many others to flee to Iran. When the coalition launched a ground attack in late February, the air war had so devastated the Iraqis that they surrendered within days.

Iraq responded to the start of the air war by launching "Scud" missiles at populated areas in Israel and Saudi Arabia. The Scuds terrorized the populations of targeted cities and killed a number of people. Analysts believe that Iraq used the attacks on Israel to try to draw it into the war. Had Israel struck back, Iraq might have succeeded in forcing Arab countries out of the coalition by portraying the war as an Arab-Israeli conflict. However, Israel did not enter the war, which made it much easier to keep the coalition together.

The first major ground battle occurred at Khafji, a small Saudi coastal town near Kuwait. The Saudis had deserted the town before the war. On January 29, Iraqi troops occupied Khafji. With U.S. help, Saudi and Qatari troops recaptured the town on January 31. By late February, the air war had reduced, through casualties and desertions, the number of Iraqi troops in Kuwait and southern Iraq to about 183,000.

At about 4 a.m. on February 24, coalition forces launched a major ground attack into Iraq and Kuwait. The attack consisted of several large operations carried out at the same time. United States and French troops invaded Iraq from Saudi Arabia, west of Iraqi fortifications in Kuwait.

This map shows the routes taken by allied ground forces in the Persian Gulf War of 1991. The ground attack included three major movements, all originating from northern Saudi Arabia. In two of them, coalition forces attacked Iraqi troops in Kuwait or southern Iraq. In the other, allied forces charged north into Iraq to cut off Iraqi supply lines.

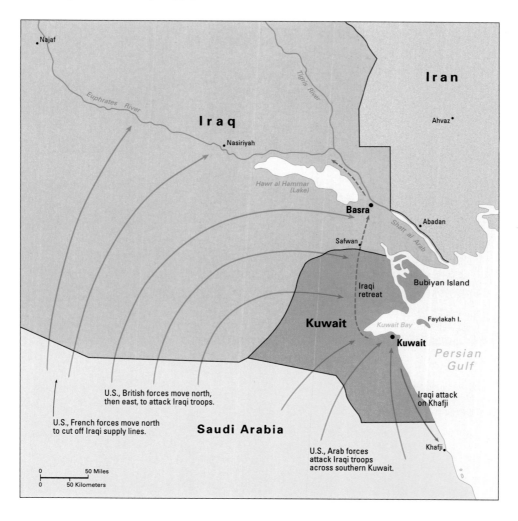

U.S. General H. Norman Schwarzkopf, U.S. Central Command, and Lieutenant General Prince Khalid bin Sultan, commander of Joint Forces in Saudi Arabia (left to right), discuss cease-fire conditions in Iraq with Iraqi generals during Operation Desert Storm in March 1991.

They moved rapidly north into Iraq and toward the Euphrates River to cut off Iraqi supply lines and to prevent an Iraqi retreat. United States and British troops also crossed into Iraq from Saudi Arabia. They moved north into Iraq and then swept east to attack the Iraqi troops.

In another operation, coalition troops assaulted Iraqi forces at several points across southern Kuwait. These coalition troops consisted of U.S. marines and troops from Egypt, Kuwait, Saudi Arabia, and Syria. The

troops quickly broke through Iraqi fortifications, and about 63,000 Iraqi soldiers surrendered. On February 26, Hussein ordered his troops to leave Kuwait. But by that time, the Iraqi forces had been surrounded. The coalition ended all military operations at 8 a.m. on February 28, about 100 hours after the ground attack had begun.

Iraq accepted the terms of a formal cease-fire agreement on April 6. On April 11, the UN Security Council officially declared an end to the war. In the agreement, Iraq promised to pay Kuwait for war damages. Iraq also agreed to destroy all its biological and chemical weapons, its facilities for producing them, and any facilities or materials it might have for producing nuclear weapons. Iraq stockpiled chemical weapons in Kuwait before the ground war, but there is no evidence that either side used chemical weapons in the war. Neither side used biological or nuclear weapons. After the cease-fire, the UN continued the embargo to pressure Iraq to carry out its promises. However, Iraq stubbornly resisted complying with the terms of the cease-fire agreement.

As many as 100,000 Iraqi troops may have died in the war, but some experts believe the total was much lower. Only about 370 coalition troops died. Thousands of civilians in Iraq and Kuwait probably were killed in the war.

Coalition bombing severely damaged Iraq's transportation systems, communication systems, and petroleum and other industries. Coalition attacks also wiped out much of Iraq's ability to provide electric power and clean water to its citizens. As a result, many civilians died after the war from disease or a lack of medicine or food.

In Kuwait, Iraqi troops looted the country and damaged many of Kuwait's oil wells, in most cases by setting them on fire. In addition, Iraq dumped some 200 million gallons (760 million liters) of Kuwaiti crude oil into the Persian Gulf, killing wildlife and causing long-term harm to the environment.

After the war

After the war, Hussein continued to rule Iraq. But revolts broke out among Kurds in northern Iraq and, in southern Iraq, among Arabs of the Shīah division of Islam. Both groups had long opposed Hussein's rule. Iraq's army swiftly put down most of the rebellions. Hundreds of thou-

Oil wells burned out of control in Kuwait after retreating Iraqi troops set fire to hundreds of wells during the Persian Gulf War of 1991. The dense smoke from the fires darkened the skies in Kuwait and caused serious air pollution in Iran, Iraq, Kuwait, and other parts of west and southwest Asia.

sands of Shī`ite Arabs then fled to Iran. Thousands of others hid in the marshlands of southern Iraq. More than a million Kurds fled to the mountains of northern Iraq and to Turkey and Iran. Tens of thousands of Kurds and Shī`ites were killed in the revolts or died later of disease, exposure, or hunger. In April 1991, the United States and other coalition members established a safety zone in northern Iraq to protect Kurdish refugees from Iraqi troops. Coalition forces remained in northern Iraq until July. But coalition aircraft continued to patrol northern Iraq as part of an effort to enforce a ban on Iraqi aircraft flights and troop movements there. In 1992, to protect the Shī`ite population, coalition forces imposed a ban on Iraqi aircraft flights over southern Iraq. In 1996, Iraqi troops attacked Kurds in northern Iraq. The United States responded with missile attacks against Iraqi military targets.

The Persian Gulf War of 1991 also focused world attention on the Arab-

Kurds

The Kurds are a people of a mountainous region of southwest Asia. Their homeland extends mainly over parts of the countries of Armenia, Iran, Iraq, Syria, and Turkey. The number of Kurds in the area has been estimated at more than 25 million. Most Kurds are Sunni Muslims. They speak Kurdish, an Indo-European language related to Persian.

Many Kurds live in rural communities. They farm and herd sheep and goats. Farm crops include cotton, tobacco, and sugar beets. Other Kurds live in cities, such as Mahabad, Sanandaj, and Bakhtaran in Iran; Arbil, Kirkuk, and As Sulaymaniyah in Iraq; and Diyarbakir and Van in Turkey. Since the late 1900's, many Kurds have migrated to large cities outside the Kurdish homeland, such as Istanbul and Ankara in Turkey.

Historically, the name *Kurdistan* (a Persian word meaning the *Land of the Kurds*) has been used for the area where the Kurds live. Today, only a small province in Iran is officially named Kurdistan.

The Kurds have never been united under a government of their own. Their desire for cultural and political independence has led to conflicts between them and the governments under which they live. Efforts to establish self-government were crushed by the Turks during World War I (1914-1918), by the Iraqis in the 1970's and 1980's, and by the Iranian government after 1979. Several thousand Kurds were killed in 1988 when Iraq attacked Kurdish villages with bombs containing poison chemicals. From 1984 to 1999, Kurdish rebels in southeastern Turkey waged a guerrilla campaign against the Turkish government.

Kurds in Iraq rebelled in March 1991, soon after Iraq's military forces were defeated in the Persian Gulf War of that year. Iraq's

This map shows the location of the Kurds' homeland. Kurds are a people of a mountainous region of southwest Asia. Their homeland extends mainly over parts of Armenia, Iran, Iraq, Syria, and Turkey. This area is historically called *Kurdistan,* a Persian word meaning *Land of the Kurds.*

army quickly put down the rebellion. In response, nations that had fought Iraq in the Persian Gulf War of 1991 created a safety zone in northern Iraq to protect the Kurds from Iraqi troops.

The Iraq War (2003-2011) brought new challenges. Kurdish officials continued to work to maintain a degree of self-rule while a new government was set up in Iraq. In April 2005, Iraq's *interim* (temporary) parliament elected Kurdish leader Jalal Talabani as interim president. In April 2006, Iraq's parliament reelected him as president. He was the first Kurdish head of any Arab country.

In northeastern Iraq, the Kurdish region is largely *autonomous* (self-ruling). In 2014, Sunni extremists pushed Iraq to the brink of civil war. As Iraqi government forces withdrew from northern Iraq, Kurdish security forces—known as *peshmerga* (Kurdish for *those who confront death*)—occupied Kirkuk. Kirkuk, an important city and traditional Kurdish capital, is just beyond the Kurds' autonomous region.

Israeli conflict. After the war, the United States renewed diplomatic efforts to resolve disputes between Israel and Arab countries. These efforts helped lead to the signing of several agreements between Israel and the Palestine Liberation Organization, a group that represents the Palestinian people.

Iraq did not fulfill the terms of the 1991 cease-fire agreement. On several occasions, Iraq failed to cooperate with UN teams sent to inspect suspected weapons sites. In the late 1990's and early 2000's, U.S. and British planes attacked targets in northern and southern Iraq many times to enforce the Iraqi flight bans and to disable Iraq's air defense systems. In 1998, Iraq began to refuse to allow UN weapons inspectors into the country.

The deceptive actions by Iraq allowed the United States to raise the specter of weapons development by Iraq a few years later. In 2002, the United States and the United Kingdom began to threaten military action against Iraq unless it fully eliminated any *weapons of mass destruction* (chemical, biological, or nuclear weapons) and any facilities for producing them. Following these threats came renewed UN weapons inspections in Iraq. While inspections were underway, the United States and the United Kingdom built momentum towards another war in Iraq.

Gulf War syndrome

After the Persian Gulf War of 1991, some veterans complained of physical and psychological ailments that they believed were related to their service. Their symptoms were sometimes referred to as Gulf War syndrome. Some people believed that exposure to dangerous chemicals when U.S. troops destroyed a chemical weapons depot in Iraq may have affected the troops. Others argued that the syndrome was not a single illness and that the symptoms resulted from the stress of war or other factors.

Gulf War syndrome symptoms include fatigue, headaches, rashes, digestive disorders, and muscle and joint pain. Veterans also report stress, depression, insomnia, and trouble remembering or concentrating. Members of the armed forces of the United Kingdom, the United States, and other nations have reported these symptoms. Although affected veterans describe similar ailments, their health problems do not match the pattern of any previously known illness. Experts have proposed several theories to explain Gulf War syndrome.

One theory is that small doses of chemical weapons may have caused Gulf War syndrome. Iraq stored large quantities of nerve gas and other deadly chemicals in weapons stockpiles. After the fighting ended, the United States and its allies bombed some storage sites to destroy Iraq's weapon reserves. This bombing may have released clouds of chemicals that drifted long distances, exposing troops to tiny amounts of deadly gases. Researchers are studying whether such low doses of chemical weapons can cause health problems.

French soldiers from the Foreign Legion infantry regiment wear gas masks as they practice nuclear, biological, and chemical training in the Saudi Desert in October 1990.

Another theory is that a combination of insecticides and a drug called pyridostigmine bromide (*PIHR uh doh STIHG meen BROH myd*) played a role in Gulf War syndrome. United States troops were given pyridostigmine bromide (often shortened to PB) experimentally to protect them against nerve gas. At the same time, soldiers used large quantities of pesticides and insect repellents to control desert pests. PB protects against nerve gas by inactivating an enzyme that also breaks down the chemicals in pesticides. As a result, some experts think that PB allowed pesticides to build up to damaging levels in the bodies of American soldiers.

In addition, troops were vaccinated against many diseases and were exposed to blowing sand, heavy smoke from burning oil wells, and other environmental hazards. Some experts believe the syndrome is chiefly a stress reaction resulting from the harsh environment, physical hardship, and constant threat of attack.

Affected veterans are frustrated by the delay in understanding Gulf War syndrome and by certain government actions regarding it. For example, the United States Department of Defense denied until 1996 that American troops might have been exposed to any chemical weapons. Researchers are gathering additional data about the health of Gulf War veterans, and more studies are planned. One study revealed that Gulf War veterans are more likely to develop amyotrophic lateral sclerosis (*uh MY uh TROF ihk LAT uhr uhl sklih ROH sihs*) than veterans who did not serve in the war. This illness, also known as ALS or Lou Gehrig's disease, is a rare, incurable disorder of the nervous system. Experts do not know why ALS is more common in Gulf War veterans and caution that Gulf War syndrome may never be conclusively explained.

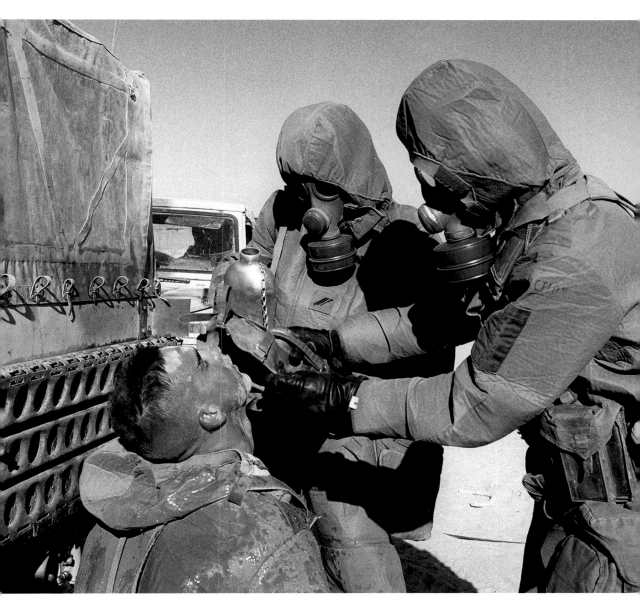

Two French paratroopers decontaminate their comrade during a chemical drill in December 1990. Members of the armed forces of the United Kingdom, the United States, and other nations complained of nervous disorders, muscular pains, and generalized fatigue after taking part in the Persian Gulf War of 1991.

The United States and its allies struggled to establish stability in Afghanistan. In this photograph, British Royal Marines scramble out of the back of a Chinook helicopter as part of Operation Buzzard in southeastern Afghanistan in July 2002. The U.K.-led operation was launched in May.

CHAPTER TWO

Afghanistan War

The Afghanistan War began in 2001. It started as a short but intense war in which the United States and its allies battled the Taliban (*TAL uh ban*), a militant Islamic group that controlled Afghanistan. International forces overthrew the Taliban regime and helped establish a new government in Afghanistan.

The conflict persisted in the years that followed, however, as the United States and its allies struggled to establish stability in the country. The war formally ended in 2014. It became the longest deployment of American combat troops in U.S. history. The Vietnam War (1957-1975) was a longer war overall, but American combat troops only served there during the period from 1965 to 1975. Since the beginning of the Afghanistan War, more than 3,500 coalition soldiers, mostly American, have died in Afghanistan.

On Sept. 11, 2001, terrorists used hijacked commercial jetliners to attack the World Trade Center in New York City and the Pentagon Building near Washington, D.C. (Hijackers crashed another jet in a Pennsylvania field.) Nearly 3,000 people were killed in the attacks. The U.S. government linked the attacks to an Islamic extremist group called al-Qa`ida (*KY ih duh*), also spelled al-Qaeda. The Taliban had hosted the group in Afghanistan since 1996. Following the attacks, U.S. President George W. Bush called for a worldwide campaign against al-Qa`ida and other international terrorist networks. The campaign was commonly called the "war on terrorism" or the "war on terror."

History of Afghanistan (pre-9/11)

About 1500 B.C., the Aryans, a central Asian people, invaded the region. Scholars believe they killed many of the area's inhabitants and intermarried with others. In the mid-500's B.C., Persians invaded northern Afghanistan, a region then called Bactria (*BAK tree uh*). The Persians ruled Bactria until about 330 B.C. when Greeks and Macedonians led by Alexander the Great (356-323 B.C.) conquered the region and much of the rest of Afghanistan.

About 246 B.C., the Bactrians revolted. They conquered much of Afghanistan and formed a kingdom that lasted about 150 years. They were conquered by the Kushans (*ku SHAHNZ*) of central Asia. Sasanians (*sa SAY nee uhnz*) from Persia invaded in the A.D. 200's, and White Huns from central Asia defeated the Kushans and Sasanians in the 400's.

Arab Muslim armies swept into parts of what is now Afghanistan during the late 600's. Three Muslim dynasties—the Tahirid (*tuh HEER ihd*), the Samanid (*suh MAH nihd*), and the Saffarid (*suh FAHR ihd*)—controlled much of the region during the 800's and 900's. Under these dynasties, most local inhabitants converted to Islam.

Turkic-speaking peoples from eastern Persia and central Asia ruled Afghanistan from about 900 to 1200. The most famous of these were the Ghaznavids (*gahz NAH vihdz*), who, under Mahmud of Ghazni (*mah MOOD ov gahz NEE*) (971-1030), conquered much of northern India. Afghanistan was conquered by Mongols led by Genghis Khan (*JEHNG gihs KAHN*) (1162?-1227) in the 1200's and by Timur (*tih MOOR* or *TIHM ur*) (1336-1405), also called Tamerlane (*TAM uhr layn*), in the 1300's. Safavids (*sa FAH veedz*) from Persia and Mughals (*MOO guhlz*) from India fought for control of Afghanistan from the mid-1500's to the early 1700's.

In 1747, Ahmad Khan Abdalli (*AH mahd KAHN ab DAHL ee*) came to power. He took the title *shah* (king) and adopted the name *Durrani*

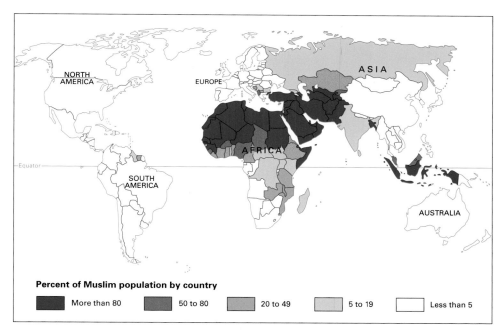

Percent of Muslim population by country

More than 80	50 to 80	20 to 49	5 to 19	Less than 5

This map shows where Muslims live throughout the world. Areas with the largest percentage of Muslims in the population include northern Africa and Southeast and Southwest Asia.

(Pearl of the Age). Ahmad Shah Durrani united the many Pashtun (*pash TOON*) tribes, establishing the Durrani Empire. This marked the beginning of modern Afghanistan, though it included territory stretching far beyond the country's current borders. Ahmad Shah established his capital at Kandahar (*KAN duh hahr*). His son and successor, Timur Shah, moved the capital from Kandahar to Kabul in 1775. Timur Shah and his successors struggled to keep the Afghans united and lost control of most of the territory beyond the current borders of Afghanistan.

In 1819, civil war broke out among rival groups that wanted to rule the country. The war lasted until 1826 when Dost Muhammad Khan (*duhst moo HAM uhd KAHN*) gained control. He took the title of *amir* (*uh MIHR*), which means *prince* or *leader*. Dost Muhammad's descendants ruled the country for the next 150 years.

For almost 200 years before the United States launched its military action against the militant Islamic group the Taliban, Afghanistan faced many periods of instability. World powers saw its geographic position as ripe for colonization. Also, far-flung areas of Afghanistan that have been difficult to control complicate governing the vast country.

During the 1800's, the United Kingdom and Russia competed for control of Afghanistan. The United Kingdom wanted to protect its empire in India, which was threatened by Russia's expansion in Afghanistan. In 1839, British Indian troops invaded Afghanistan to stop Russia's perceived influence in the region. The invasion set off the First Anglo-Afghan War, which lasted until the British withdrew in 1842.

In 1878, the United Kingdom invaded Afghanistan again, starting the

In 1839, British Indian troops invaded Afghanistan to stop Russia's perceived influence in the region. The invasion set off the First Anglo-Afghan War.

Second Anglo-Afghan War. The British found it difficult to establish control of the country. They recognized Abdur Rahman Khan (*ahb DOOR rah MAN KAHN*) as amir in 1880, though his authority was limited to the country's internal affairs. In return, Abdur Rahman accepted British India's control of Afghanistan's foreign relations. Often called the "Iron Amir," he strengthened the national government and reduced the power of tribal leaders. After he died in 1901, his policies were continued by his son Habibullah Khan (*hah BEE boo LAH KAHN*).

Early in 1919, Habibullah Khan was assassinated. One of his sons, Amanullah Khan (*uh mah NUHL ah KAHN*), then became amir and attacked British troops in India, beginning the Third Anglo-Afghan War. The United Kingdom had just finished fighting in World War I (1914-1918). After a brief conflict, it decided to end its involvement in Afghanistan. In August 1919, Afghanistan became fully independent.

Amanullah began many reforms, challenging long-held traditions and customs. The nation's first constitution was adopted in 1923, and Amanullah changed his title from amir to shah in 1926. But tribal and religious leaders resisted the reform movement and forced Amanullah Shah to give up the throne in 1929.

Late in 1929, Muhammad Nadir Shah (*moo HAM uhd nah DIHR SHAH*) became king. In 1931, Afghanistan adopted a new constitution, under which Nadir Shah planned a program of gradual reform. But he was assassinated in 1933 before many of the reforms were begun. Muhammad Zahir Shah (*moo HAM uhd ZAH heer SHAH*), Nadir Shah's son, then became king.

Afghanistan avoided involvement in World War II (1939-1945). By the early 1950's, Afghanistan had developed good relations with the United States and many Western European nations. But the Afghans feared the intentions of the Soviet Union, their country's powerful Communist neighbor. In 1953, Muhammad Daoud Khan (*moo HAM uhd dah OOD KAHN*), the king's cousin and brother-in-law, took control of the government and made himself prime minister. Under Daoud, Afghanistan took no side in the Cold War (1945-1991), a period of hostility between Communist and non-Communist nations. The country received aid from both the United States and the Soviet Union.

Border disputes with Pakistan and other problems led to pressures that forced Daoud to resign in 1963. In 1964, under the leadership of Zahir Shah and Western-educated scholars and thinkers, Afghanistan adopted a constitution that provided for a democratic government for the first time. But many problems arose. Zahir Shah and the legislature could not agree on the role of political parties within the reform program. Parliament often deadlocked on key issues. As a result, the new democratic system failed to bring about the progress that the framers of Afghanistan's constitution had hoped for.

In 1973, Daoud overthrew Zahir Shah. He established the Republic of Afghanistan and assumed the offices of president and prime minister. In 1978, the People's Democratic Party of Afghanistan (PDPA), the country's Communist party, overthrew Daoud, who was killed in the uprising. The PDPA established a Communist government.

Many in Afghanistan opposed the new government. They believed the government's policies conflicted with the teachings of Islam. In addition, they resented Soviet influence on the government. A widespread rebellion against the government soon broke out.

The Soviet Union worried that the rebels, who called themselves *mujahideen* (*moo JAH huh deen*) (holy warriors), might defeat the Afghan government forces. On Dec. 25, 1979, the Soviet Union invaded Afghanistan. Over the next decade, the Soviet Union sent more than 100,000 troops to join the fight against the rebels. The Soviets had far better equipment than their opponents. But the rebels were supplied by countries opposed to the Soviet Union, including the United States and Saudi Arabia. The mujahideen used guerrilla tactics to overcome the Soviet advantage. The countryside suffered most from the war. The Soviets and Afghan government forces bombed many villages.

In 1988 and 1989, the Soviet Union withdrew its troops from Afghanistan. But the fighting between the mujahideen and government forces continued until 1992, when the rebels overthrew the government. In the need for steady leadership, the Taliban rose to power, maintaining an Islamist rule until the U.S. invasion in 2001.

Afghans cheer as Soviet troops, shown here in tanks, retreat from Kabul, Afghanistan, in 1988. The Soviet Union invaded Afghanistan in 1979 and 1980 to support the Communist government there. Despite their superior military strength, the Soviets failed to defeat the Afghan rebels, known as *mujahideen*.

The Taliban

The Taliban is a militant Sunni (*SOON ee*) Islamic political group. The group gained control of most of Afghanistan in the mid-1990's and sought to turn Afghanistan into an Islamic state.

In 2001, the United States and its allies helped Afghan opposition forces, known collectively as the Northern Alliance, topple the Taliban. However, the Taliban have remained active in the region. The word *taliban* (also spelled *taleban*) means *seekers after knowledge*. The name refers to the group's origin in Islamic schools.

While in control of Afghanistan, the Taliban enforced strict adherence to their interpretation of Islamic laws and practices. These included restrictions on most modern forms of entertainment, as well as on dress and personal grooming. For example, the Taliban forced men to grow beards and women to wear veils. Those who violated the Taliban's law were severely punished.

The Taliban formed in 1994. The group sought to end the lawlessness that had resulted from years of war in Afghanistan. From 1979 to 1989, the Soviet Union occupied Afghanistan to support the country's pro-Communist government against rebels. After the Soviet forces withdrew, Afghanistan descended into civil war as various factions vied for power.

With assistance from Pakistan's military, security, and intelligence services, the Taliban captured Afghanistan's second largest city, Kandahar, in 1994. Throughout 1995, Taliban rebels strengthened their position in southern Afghanistan. A year later, they seized Afghanistan's capital and largest city, Kabul.

In 1998, the United States accused the Taliban of harboring the Saudi-born millionaire Osama bin Laden. U.S. authorities linked bin Laden to terrorist attacks against two U.S. embassies in Africa that year. The United States launched missile strikes against suspected terrorist training camps in Afghanistan. A Taliban spokesman acknowledged that bin Laden was in Afghanistan as a guest of the Taliban.

The United States accused bin Laden and al-Qa`ida, his terrorist organization, of planning the Sept. 11, 2001, attacks on the World Trade Center in New York City and the Pentagon Building near Washington, D.C. Nearly 3,000 people died. U.S. officials demanded the Taliban surrender bin Laden. The Taliban refused. The United States and its allies then launched a massive military campaign against al-Qa`ida in October.

The Taliban fell from power in late 2001. Many surviving Taliban and Qa`ida members fled to northern Pakistan, where they regrouped. From safe havens along the border, the Taliban have launched attacks against Afghan government forces and their allies from the United States and the North Atlantic Treaty Organization (NATO), as well as Pakistani politicians and others. The United States began to use unpiloted aircraft called *drones* to combat the Taliban in Pakistan. In 2011, U.S. military forces killed bin Laden in Pakistan. In 2015, the Taliban confirmed that long-time leader, Mullah Omar (*MUHL uh OH mahr*), had been dead since 2013.

9/11 and the war on terror

The September 11 attacks of 2001, commonly called 9/11, were the worst acts of terrorism ever carried out against the United States. On that Tuesday morning, terrorists hijacked four commercial jetliners and crashed two of them into the twin towers of the World Trade Center in New York City, and one into the Pentagon Building near Washington, D.C. Hijackers crashed the fourth jet in a Pennsylvania field to prevent it from being reclaimed by passengers. The attacks killed about 3,000 people, including the 19 hijackers.

The U.S. government linked the attacks to al-Qaʾida, an Islamic extremist group founded by the Saudi-born millionaire Osama bin Laden. Bin Laden had previously issued a *fatwa* (religious edict) calling for Muslims to kill Americans, and al-Qaʾida—which means *the base* in Arabic—had targeted U.S. interests on several occasions. It attacked U.S.

On Sept. 11, 2001, at an elementary school classroom in Sarasota, Florida, U.S. President George W. Bush (seated) receives information that two planes had struck the World Trade Center in New York City earlier that morning. The president was speaking with a group of students at the school when the terrorist attacks occurred.

military housing in Saudi Arabia in 1996, U.S. embassies in Kenya and Tanzania in 1998, and the U.S. Navy warship *Cole* in Yemen in 2000. Al-Qaʿida sought to drive U.S. forces from Saudi Arabia—home to Mecca and Medina, the holy cities of Islam—and from other parts of the Persian Gulf region. Many scholars believe that the group hoped to unite the Islamic world against the United States and its allies and to establish a worldwide society of Muslims governed by Shariʿah (strict Islamic law).

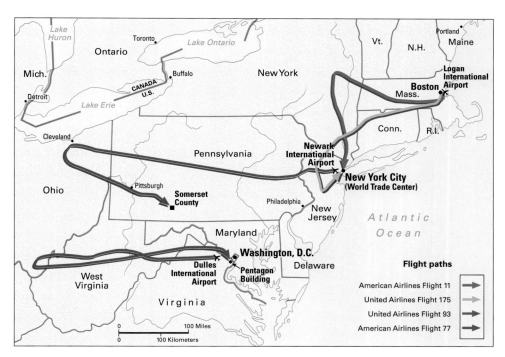

This map shows the flight paths of the four hijacked airplanes involved in the terrorist attacks of Sept. 11, 2001. American Airlines Flight 11 and United Airlines Flight 175, both headed from Boston to Los Angeles, were diverted to strike the twin towers of the World Trade Center in New York City. United Airlines Flight 93, headed from Newark International Airport in New Jersey to San Francisco, crashed in a field in southwestern Pennsylvania. American Airlines Flight 77, which left Dulles International Airport just outside of Washington, D.C., and was bound for Los Angeles, crashed into the Pentagon Building.

On the morning of Sept. 11, 2001, hijackers crashed jetliners into the twin towers of the World Trade Center in New York City. After the north tower, right, was struck, a second plane headed for the south tower. Thousands of people died in the attacks.

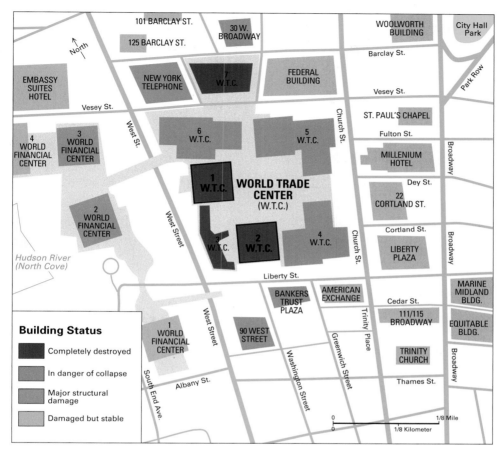

The World Trade Center complex originally consisted of seven buildings. This map shows the degree of damage to the buildings within and around the center after the attacks.

On Sept. 18, 2001, U.S. President George W. Bush signed a joint resolution of the United States Congress giving the president the "Authorization for Use of Military Force" against the nations or organizations responsible for the attacks. In a speech two days later, Bush called for a "war on terror" to destroy international terrorist networks. "Our war on terror begins with al-Qa`ida, but it does not end there," he said. "It will

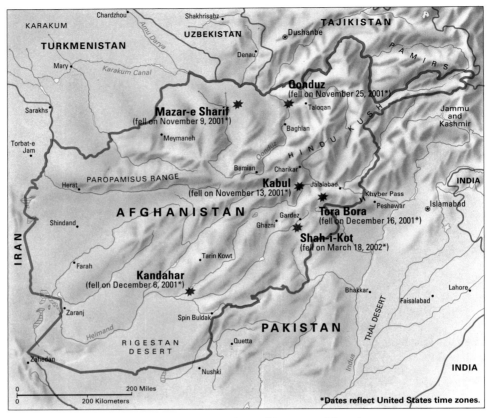

Military strikes against al-Qaʿida and the Taliban in Afghanistan began in October 2001. The United States and its allies launched a powerful air campaign and supported Afghan rebel groups to drive the Taliban from power. This map shows the locations of major battles in Afghanistan.

not end until every terrorist group of global reach has been found, stopped, and defeated."

Afghanistan was a major focus of the "war on terrorism" campaign. That country's ruling group, the Taliban, had hosted al-Qaʿida. The United States demanded that the Taliban shut down Qaʿida training camps in the country and arrest Qaʿida leaders, including bin Laden.

When the Taliban refused to do so, the United States and its allies launched a military campaign.

The military campaign, called Operation Enduring Freedom, began on Oct. 7, 2001, with a series of U.S. and British air strikes against Taliban positions. Early in the conflict, the United States sent military special operations teams and agents from the Central Intelligence Agency (CIA) into Afghanistan. In November, American Marines joined them. Afghan anti-Taliban forces, including an association called the Northern Alliance, fought on the ground. The anti-Taliban groups received assistance from United States and other allied forces.

Throughout November, the Afghan anti-Taliban forces established control over major cities and towns, including Kabul, Afghanistan's capital and largest city. Kandahar was the last major city to fall. Afghan

Afghans cheered the arrival of Northern Alliance rebel troops in Kabul, Afghanistan's capital, on Nov. 13, 2001. Northern Alliance and United States military forces drove the oppressive Taliban regime out of the city.

Osama bin Laden

Osama bin Laden (1957?-2011) was a Saudi-born millionaire and radical Muslim who supported international terrorism. He opposed many U.S. policies in the Middle East, particularly U.S. support for Israel, as well as the presence of U.S. troops in Saudi Arabia from 1991 to 2003. He also opposed Muslim governments that were allied to the United States. Bin Laden was the founder and leader of al-Qaʿida, a global terrorist organization that is allied with other Muslim extremist groups worldwide. On May 2, 2011 (May 1 in the United States), U.S. military forces killed bin Laden in Abbottabad, Pakistan.

United States and other Western intelligence officials believed bin Laden was the mastermind behind several terrorist attacks against U.S. targets, including U.S. embassies in Kenya and Tanzania in 1998. In September 2001, U.S. government officials named him as the prime suspect in the attacks that month on the World Trade Center in New York City and the Pentagon Building near Washington, D.C. Thousands of people died in the attacks.

Bin Laden was born in Riyadh (*ree YAHD*), Saudi Arabia, to a wealthy family. He studied civil engineering and management at King Abdulaziz University in Jiddah (*JIH duh*). In 1979, he left Saudi Arabia to join the mujahideen in Pakistan who were fighting against the Soviet occupation of Afghanistan. The mujahideen were Muslims from many countries, especially Arab countries, who became guerrillas in what they considered a *jihad* (*jih HAHD*), or holy war, against the Soviets. Bin Laden reportedly participated in several battles. Many of the Arab mujahideen eventually became associated with al-Qa`ida. Bin Laden founded al-Qa`ida in the late 1980's to resist the Soviet occupation of Afghanistan.

In 1990, Iraq invaded Kuwait. The invasion led to the Persian Gulf War of 1991. A U.S.-led military coalition sent troops to Saudi Arabia to protect that country from Iraqi invasion and to drive the Iraqis out of Kuwait. Bin Laden opposed the Saudi government's decision to allow U.S. troops in Saudi Arabia, where the holiest Muslim sites are located. He called for removal of foreign influence from Muslim countries. Because of his activities against the Saudi government, he was forced to seek asylum outside of Saudi Arabia. In 1996, he moved to Afghanistan, where he was protected by the Taliban, a conservative Islamic group that controlled most of that country.

In 1998, following the terrorist bombings of the U.S. embassies, the United States launched missile strikes against Qa`ida training camps in Afghanistan. After the September 2001 terrorist attacks, the United States demanded that the Taliban hand over bin Laden and shut down the training camps. The Taliban refused. The United States and its allies then launched military strikes in support of Afghan rebels who opposed the Taliban. The military campaign drove the Taliban from power later in 2001.

After the fall of the Taliban, U.S. and allied forces continued to search for bin Laden and other Qa`ida leaders. Many of the leaders were captured or killed. After nearly 10 years, U.S. intelligence traced bin Laden to a heavily guarded compound in Abbottabad. After a brief firefight, he was shot and killed and later buried at sea.

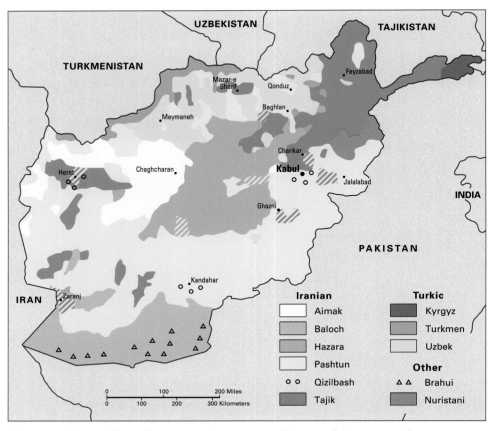

This map shows where the major ethnic groups live in Afghanistan. The Aimak, Baloch, Hazara, Pashtun, Qizilbash, and Tajik ethnic groups speak Iranian languages. These groups reside in most parts of the country. The Kyrgyz, Turkmen, and Uzbek groups speak Turkic languages. These groups reside in the northern regions of Afghanistan. The Brahui and the Nuristani ethnic groups live in southern and northeastern Afghanistan, respectively.

forces established their control of the city on December 9, bringing Taliban rule in Afghanistan to an end. The Taliban fell exactly nine weeks after the bombing began. However, the Afghanistan War did not end.

Some members of the Taliban and al-Qa`ida fled to the remote mountains along Afghanistan's eastern border with Pakistan. American officials believed Osama bin Laden was among those hiding in a mountainous region known as Tora Bora. However, the United States held back from a full-scale attack on Tora Bora. American officials were concerned that the area was too heavily fortified and that they did not have enough troops available. At that point, the United States had begun preparations to invade Iraq. The American decision to limit its attack at Tora Bora became highly controversial.

American jets bombed the Tora Bora region that December. Troops then searched the area for bin Laden, but they were unable to find him. The hunt for bin Laden continued for the next 10 years.

A new government in Afghanistan

From late November to early December 2001, the United Nations sponsored a meeting in Bonn, Germany. Delegates from Afghanistan's main ethnic and regional groups gathered to organize a temporary government. The delegates selected Hamid Karzai (*HAH mihd KAHR zy*), a member of the Popalzai (*poh PAHL zy*) tribe of the Pashtun ethnic group, to head the temporary government.

Later in December, the UN established the International Security Assistance Force (ISAF) to lead foreign forces providing security for the new Afghan government in and around the capital city of Kabul. Later, the UN expanded the ISAF's activity to other parts of Afghanistan. Eventually, about 50 countries, including every member of the North Atlantic Treaty Organization (NATO), sent troops to Afghanistan.

In early 2002, U.S. military officials believed that Taliban and Qa`ida fighters were regrouping in the Shah-i-Kot Valley, about 80 miles (130 kilometers) south of Kabul. On March 2, American forces began a campaign to prevent the Taliban from using the region to prepare attacks elsewhere in the country. By mid-March, American forces had reclaimed

Hamid Karzai

Hamid Karzai *(HAH mihd KAHR zy)* (1957-   ) was the president of Afghanistan from 2001 to 2014. He worked to establish a new national government and to control the country's warring regional leaders after the 2001 overthrow of a militant Islamic group called the Taliban, which had controlled the country since the mid-1990's. Karzai also sought international aid to help rebuild Afghanistan after many years of war. Karzai is a prominent member of the Popalzai (also spelled Popolzai or Populzai), an important tribe of the country's large Pashtun ethnic group.

Karzai was born on Dec. 24, 1957, in Kandahar. His grandfather Abdul Ahad Karzai once served as president of Afghanistan's national council. His father, also named Abdul Ahad Karzai, once served as speaker of the Afghan parliament.

During the 1980's, Hamid Karzai was active in the war against the Soviet Union, which had sent thousands of troops to Afghanistan in 1979 and 1980. Karzai served as a political representative for anti-Soviet Afghan fighters. The Soviet Union withdrew its troops in 1988 and 1989. A new government came to power in Afghanistan in 1992, with Karzai as deputy foreign minister.

Karzai initially supported the Taliban when they gained control of Afghanistan in the 1990's. However, he withdrew his support over concerns about the influence of Arab and Pakistani extremists within the Taliban. In 1999, Karzai's father was assassinated, reportedly by the Taliban.

In October 2001, a coalition of countries led by the United States attacked Afghanistan. The coalition believed that the Taliban were protecting Osama bin Laden, the leader of al-Qa`ida, a terrorist organization that supports the activities of Muslim extremists around the world. The coalition blamed al-Qa`ida for the Sept. 11, 2001, attacks on the World Trade Center in New York City and the Pentagon Building near Washington, D.C.

Karzai rallied tribes in southern Afghanistan to fight against the Taliban. He also played an important role in the coalition's victory in Kandahar, the Afghan city that was the spiritual center of Taliban activities. The coalition and its Afghan allies succeeded in driving the Taliban from power in late 2001.

Karzai became the leader of Afghanistan in December 2001 when a conference of Afghan delegates chose him to head a six-month temporary administration. In June 2002, a traditional Afghan council called a *loya jirga* (*LOY uh JEER guh*) elected Karzai to serve as president of a two-year transitional government. In January 2004, another loya jirga adopted a permanent constitution for Afghanistan. In an October 2004 presidential election, Karzai was elected president for a five-year term.

Karzai claimed victory after a presidential election in August 2009, but a United Nations-backed investigation found many voting irregularities. A runoff election was scheduled for November. However, Karzai's opponent withdrew his bid after expressing doubts that the runoff would be free of voting irregularities. Election officials then declared that, since Karzai had won the most votes in the original election, he had won the presidency.

the region, and the surviving Taliban and Qaʾida fighters had fled the valley.

In May 2003, U.S. Secretary of Defense Donald Rumsfeld told the U.S. Congress that "major combat" in Afghanistan was over. At the time, about 8,000 American troops were stationed in Afghanistan. That August, NATO took command of the ISAF. In January 2004, the transitional Afghan government adopted the country's first democratic

Election workers count ballot papers at a counting center in Kabul on Oct. 26, 2004. Hamid Karzai was elected president of Afghanistan for a five-year term.

constitution. Elections were held in October 2004, and Karzai was elected president.

Despite steps toward democracy and billions of dollars in foreign aid, the war dragged on. Fighters loyal to the Taliban and al-Qa`ida had taken refuge in the south and east of Afghanistan, and across the border in Pakistan. In 2003, insurgents began launching attacks on U.S. and allied forces from bases in Pakistan. The attacks increased over the next several years. To maintain security, the United States and its allies increased the number of troops in Afghanistan. By 2005, American forces in Afghanistan numbered nearly 20,000.

Counterinsurgency

Since 2002, Taliban and Qa`ida militants had been staging ambushes, planting explosives, carrying out suicide bomb attacks, and using other guerrilla tactics against the United States military and its allies. In addition, insurgents attacked Afghan and Pakistani politicians and other leaders who opposed their efforts. The insurgents favored the use of homemade bombs known as *improvised explosive devices* (IED's). Although such explosives were made by amateurs, they were often powerful enough to destroy heavily armored vehicles and cause severe injuries and death.

As the guerrilla attacks increased, the allied forces placed more emphasis on what is called *counterinsurgency* warfare. Counterinsurgency is military action against guerrillas and other insurgents. Allied forces in Afghanistan established outposts throughout much of the country. The allies worked to convince Afghan civilians not to support the insurgents. Troops provided security for villages and performed such humanitarian tasks as digging wells, building schools and roads, and providing medical care. Through the first decade of the 2000's, the counterinsurgency effort required large numbers of troops.

An unconventional war

The Bush administration faced the question of how to manage the detention, interrogation, and potential prosecution of captured terror suspects. Bush called the suspects "illegal combatants," a status that disqualified them from protections given to traditional prisoners of war under the Geneva Conventions. In 2002, many terrorist suspects were moved to a detention center at a United States naval base at Guantánamo Bay in Cuba.

The campaign to oust the Taliban had many of the characteristics of a conventional war. Beyond Afghanistan, however, the "war on terror" differed greatly from traditional warfare. In general, the enemy operated in secret, did not have traditional bases, and did not use conventional military tactics. American counterterror strategy soon centered on the use of *preemptive* military strikes—that is, aggressive strikes intended to prevent future attacks. American efforts included the use of unmanned aerial vehicles (UAVs) called *drones*. Drones fired on suspected terrorists in remote areas of Afghanistan, Pakistan, Somalia, Yemen, and elsewhere.

Many critics opposed the use of drone attacks. In some cases, civilians have been killed in drone attacks after they were mistaken for enemy fighters. Additional controversy stemmed from the use of drones in regions where allied forces were not authorized. The U.S. and allied air teams repeatedly used drones to attack targets they believed to be Taliban and Qa'ida strongholds in Pakistan. Many Pakistanis opposed the use of drone strikes in their country.

The UN and other international organizations have estimated that thousands of Afghan civilians have been killed by allied airstrikes—

U.S. soldiers board a Chinook helicopter to return to Kandahar Army Air Field in 2003. They were searching for Taliban fighters and illegal weapons caches in the Daychopan district in Afghanistan.

both by drones and piloted aircraft—during the course of the war. The killing of Afghan civilians has contributed to criticism of the United States and caused tension between U.S. and Afghan leaders. However, the UN has noted that a vast majority of the civilian deaths in the war have been caused by the Taliban and al-Qa`ida.

U.S. security and antiterrorism policies

Following 9/11, the U.S. government sought to increase its ability to investigate and detain suspected terrorists. In October 2001, Congress passed the Patriot Act. The act gave law enforcement the power to detain any noncitizen suspected of being a risk to national security. It also granted authorities greater freedom to conduct searches and use

People protest against the Patriot Act, passed in October 2001. Critics argued that the law threatened civil liberties and violated constitutional protections against unreasonable searches and seizures.

wiretapping (the interception of communication through electronic listening devices). Critics argued that the law threatened civil liberties and violated constitutional protections against unreasonable searches and seizures. When Congress renewed the act in 2006, it included new safeguards to protect civil liberties.

In mid-September 2001, President Bush announced the creation of a new federal Office of Homeland Security to oversee the protection of the United States. In 2002, Congress expanded the office into a new executive department, the Department of Homeland Security.

In 2004, Congress passed the Intelligence Reform and Terrorism Prevention Act, which reorganized the U.S. government's intelligence community. The act created the Office of the Director of National Intelligence to coordinate intelligence collection, analysis, and sharing among agencies.

Many civil rights activists argued that the Patriot Act and other antiterror policies gave the government too much power and threatened individuals' privacy and civil rights. Critics also targeted drone programs. Many observers cited reports that civilian casualties caused by drone strikes often led to increases in terrorist recruitment. In addition, some critics argued that intelligence gained through brutal interrogation techniques had little or no value.

Surveillance programs conducted by the National Security Agency (NSA)—an agency within the U.S. Department of Defense—became the subject of international controversy in 2013. That year, NSA contractor Edward Snowden revealed documents showing that the NSA spied on both U.S. allied and enemy countries around the world.

In 2013, National Security Agency (NSA) contractor Edward Snowden revealed documents showing that the NSA spied on both U.S. allied and enemy countries around the world.

U.S. relations with Pakistan

Pakistan became an important U.S. ally in the Afghanistan War. Afghanistan is a land-locked country, so the United States and its allies used the Pakistani port of Karachi (*kuh RAH chee*) as a transportation hub for equipment and supplies. NATO trucks carried supplies from Karachi into northwestern Pakistan, and across the border into Afghanistan. However, the war also strained Pakistan's relationship with the United States.

A low point in relations between the United States and Pakistan came in late 2011, after a U.S. airstrike killed Pakistani troops stationed along the border with Afghanistan. For several months, Pakistani forces blocked the road that NATO was using to transport supplies into Afghanistan.

Some international affairs experts accused Pakistan's leaders of harboring top Qa`ida figures, including Osama bin Laden. Pakistan denied the allegations. However, American intelligence tracked bin Laden to a heavily guarded compound in Abbottabad, a Pakistani city northeast of Islamabad. A U.S. special forces team killed bin Laden there on May 2, 2011 (May 1 in the United States).

President Obama's national security team gathered at the White House in May 2011 to monitor the raid that killed terrorist leader Osama bin Laden. The team included Vice President Joe Biden, seated at left; Obama, in black jacket; and Admiral Mike Mullen, chairman of the Joint Chiefs of Staff, standing (wearing dark necktie). Secretary of State Hillary Clinton and Secretary of Defense Robert Gates are seated at the right.

In 2014, the Senate Intelligence Committee released a report examining the interrogation practices used by the CIA in the years after 9/11. The report documented numerous brutal practices. It also found that the CIA routinely misled the White House about the effectiveness of such methods in uncovering terror plots.

In the years following 9/11, CIA agents working overseas often flew terror suspects to secret CIA-run prisons or transferred them to the custody of foreign governments. The practice of sending terror suspects to foreign or secret prisons to be interrogated became known as *extraordinary rendition*. In their quest to uncover information, CIA agents

In 2002, many al-Qa`ida and Taliban terrorist suspects (in orange jumpsuits) were moved to a detention center at a United States naval base at Guantánamo Bay in Cuba.

subjected many suspects to brutal interrogation practices. Such practices included waterboarding—a technique in which suspects are made to believe that they are drowning.

Barack Obama succeeded Bush as president of the United States in 2009. Obama sought to recast the ways the nation addressed the terror threat. "We must define our effort not as a boundless 'global war on terror,'" he said, "but rather as a series of persistent, targeted efforts to dismantle specific networks of violent extremists that threaten America." Obama sought to close the prison at Guantánamo Bay, and he banned the use of controversial interrogation tactics that many critics had described as torture. Critics of counterterrorism programs contended, however, that little had changed under the new president. They noted that Obama had maintained surveillance programs begun under Bush and expanded the use of drone strikes against terror suspects.

End of U.S. combat missions in Afghanistan

In mid-2011, NATO began transferring national peacekeeping and security duties to Afghan forces. The transfer was complete in June 2013. By that time, Afghan security and military forces had been granted leadership over security operations for the entire country. International troops shifted into a supporting role.

In February 2013, President Obama announced that the United States would end the war in Afghanistan by the close of 2014. He later an-

nounced that nearly 10,000 American troops would remain in Afghanistan through 2016, serving in such noncombat roles as training Afghan soldiers, advising Afghan army units, and helping maintain equipment.

In September 2014, the Afghan government signed a security agreement with the U.S. government that clarified the terms under which American troops would remain in Afghanistan. In December, NATO and the United States formally ended their combat missions in Afghanistan. On Dec. 28, 2014, the United States held a ceremony in Kabul to mark the formal end of the war. However, the Taliban increased their presence in Afghanistan in 2015, and security forces continued to battle the insurgents. U.S. troops have remained in Afghanistan as American leaders seek a solution to the war.

U.S. General John Campbell speaks during a ceremony marking the end of the International Security Assistance Force's (ISAF) combat mission in Afghanistan at ISAF headquarters in Kabul on Dec. 28, 2014. It marked the formal end of the Afghanistan war. However, U.S. troops have remained in Afghanistan as American leaders seek a solution to the war.

Explosions caused by a missile strike rock one of the palaces of the Iraqi leader Saddam Hussein in Baghdad. The city lies on the west bank of the Tigris River, in the foreground. Air attacks by the U.S.-led forces in 2003 hit strategic targets throughout Iraq.

CHAPTER THREE

Iraq War

The Iraq War began when the United States and its allies launched an invasion of Iraq in March 2003. The U.S.-led forces controlled most of Iraq by mid-April, after the fall of the Iraqi government of Saddam Hussein. The troops involved in the invasion came mainly from the United States, though forces from the United Kingdom and a few other countries also participated.

United States President George W. Bush declared an end to major combat operations in Iraq on May 1, 2003. Afterward, U.S., Iraqi, and allied forces from many countries tried to maintain security, restore stability, and rebuild the country. However, Iraqi and foreign militants carried out many attacks against these military and security forces, as well as against civilian targets. Most of the militants opposed the presence of U.S. and allied foreign forces in Iraq. The Iraq War was a major challenge in the presidency of Barack Obama, who took office in 2009.

The U.S. government referred to the war as Operation Iraqi Freedom until the end of combat operations on Aug. 31, 2010. From Sept. 1, 2010, until the official end of the war on Dec. 15, 2011, the war was known as Operation New Dawn.

Background to the war

A coalition of 39 nations, organized mainly by the United States and the United Nations, defeated Iraq in the Persian Gulf War of 1991. That war had erupted after Hussein's forces invaded and occupied Kuwait,

Iraq's neighbor to the south, in 1990. After the invasion, the United Nations Security Council had authorized the coalition to expel Iraq from Kuwait.

As part of the cease-fire agreement that ended the Persian Gulf War of 1991, Iraq agreed to destroy all of its weapons of mass destruction and any facilities it had for producing such weapons. However, in the years following the war, Iraq did not fully comply with the terms of the agreement. On several occasions, it failed to cooperate with UN teams sent to inspect suspected weapons sites. Starting in 1998, the Iraqi government refused to allow UN weapons inspectors into the country.

In 2001 and 2002, President Bush repeatedly claimed that Hussein and his government were a threat to the security of the United States and other countries. The Bush administration accused Hussein of illegally developing and possessing weapons of mass destruction. It also charged Hussein's regime with supporting international terrorist organizations, including al-Qa`ida, the group responsible for the terrorist attacks in the United States on Sept. 11, 2001. However, many experts doubted that there was any working relationship between Iraq and al-Qa`ida.

In 2002, Bush urged the UN to compel Iraq to destroy any weapons of mass destruction it had. After the Persian Gulf War of 1991, Iraq had agreed to destroy such weapons. But since 1998, Hussein had refused to allow UN weapons inspection teams into the country to verify the destruction of the weapons.

Bush said that if the UN failed to force Iraq to disarm, the United States might launch a military attack against the country. In response, Iraq began negotiating conditions for a return of the UN weapons inspectors. Meanwhile, Bush asked the United States Congress to pass a resolution allowing him to authorize the use of military force against Iraq. Congress approved the resolution in October 2002. In November,

A British Marine fires a missile at an Iraqi position in southern Iraq while another soldier watches during the initial combat phase of the Iraq War. A coalition of forces led by the United States launched the war against Iraq in March 2003.

the UN Security Council passed a resolution demanding the resumption of weapons inspections and threatening serious consequences if Iraq failed to follow UN terms on disarmament. Iraq agreed to allow UN weapons inspectors to return to the country later that month. However, in the months that followed, the United States, the United Kingdom, and other countries charged that Hussein was not cooperating with the inspectors. The United States maintained its threat of possible military action against Iraq for resisting disarmament.

Later, Bush charged that Iraq was resisting disarmament. He asked the UN Security Council to set a deadline for Iraq to disarm. The Council members did not agree on a resolution, however. In early 2003, Bush and the leaders of the United Kingdom and Spain asked the Security Council to pass a resolution approving military action against Iraq. However, key members of the Security Council—including France, Germany, Russia, and China—refused to approve such action, arguing for more time to seek a diplomatic solution. The United States decided to move toward war despite the disagreement among the Security Council members.

Military action

On March 17, 2003 (U.S. time), Bush stated that if Hussein and his sons did not leave Iraq within 48 hours, the United States would begin military action. Hussein did not leave, and a U.S.-led coalition launched an attack on Iraq on March 20 (March 19 in the United States). The coalition consisted mostly of U.S. troops, with British, Australian, Polish, and Danish forces also participating. The removal of Hussein from power was a central goal of the military operation.

Most Americans supported Bush's decision to go to war. However, Bush also received much criticism for the decision, especially from outside the United States. Some people argued that the United States had violated international law by invading a nation that did not pose an immediate threat. Bush defended the move by describing it as a *preemptive* (preventive) action. He said the war was launched to prevent Hussein from supplying weapons of mass destruction to terrorist groups. The terrorists might then attack the United States or other countries.

A Tomahawk Land Attack Missile leaves the deck of the guided missile cruiser USS *Bunker Hill* toward military targets in Iraq on March 20, 2003, at sea in the Persian Gulf. The U.S.-led coalition was reportedly aimed at eliminating Iraqi leadership in Baghdad, Iraq's capital. In the days that followed, the coalition carried out intense bombing aimed at key targets in Baghdad and elsewhere.

Bush also argued that Hussein was a ruthless dictator who should be removed from power.

The coalition's initial attack, an air strike on March 20, was reportedly aimed at eliminating Iraqi leadership in Baghdad, Iraq's capital. In the days that followed, the coalition carried out intense bombing aimed at key targets in Baghdad and elsewhere. Many coalition ground troops invaded from the south, traveling from Kuwait toward Baghdad. The Turkish government refused to allow coalition troops to enter Iraq from Turkey, blocking the coalition's plan to launch a major offensive from the north. Instead, coalition troops parachuted into northern Iraq and there joined Iraqi Kurds, an ethnic minority, in fighting Iraqi government troops. Coalition forces in the north also targeted Ansar al-Islam, an Islamic militant group that the U.S. government said was linked to al-Qa`ida.

As coalition forces neared Baghdad, they engaged in battle with Iraq's Republican Guard, the most highly trained branch of Iraq's military. In early April, coalition forces seized control of the international airport outside Baghdad. Within days, the forces gained control of Hussein's presidential palaces and other key locations in the city. Meanwhile, coalition air strikes continued to target high-level Iraqi officials and other strategic targets both inside and outside Baghdad. On April 9, 2003, coalition forces took control of central Baghdad, and U.S. officials declared that the Hussein government had been removed from power.

Shortly before Baghdad's fall, British forces had seized control of Basra, the largest city in southern Iraq. By mid-April, coalition forces held all of Iraq's major cities. On May 1, Bush declared that major combat operations in Iraq had ended.

Coalition forces captured or killed several key officials of the Hussein regime. In July 2003, Hussein's sons, Uday and Qusay, who had held high-ranking positions in their father's government, were killed during a firefight with U.S. troops. On Dec. 13, 2003, Saddam Hussein himself was captured by U.S. troops near his hometown of Tikrit. He had been in hiding since the war began in March. In 2006, a special Iraqi court convicted Hussein of ordering the massacre of over 140 Shi`ites in 1982 and sentenced him to death by hanging. Hussein was executed by Iraqi authorities on Dec. 30, 2006. At the time, Hussein was facing additional charges, including genocide and crimes against humanity, for other actions he took while he was president of Iraq.

The collapse of Hussein's Iraqi government and the execution of the country's longtime leader did not signify the end of the operations by the U.S. and its allies. Coalition forces remained in Iraq to fight off militants and ensure security of the country. After the fall of the Hussein regime, the Bush administration then turned to the work of helping

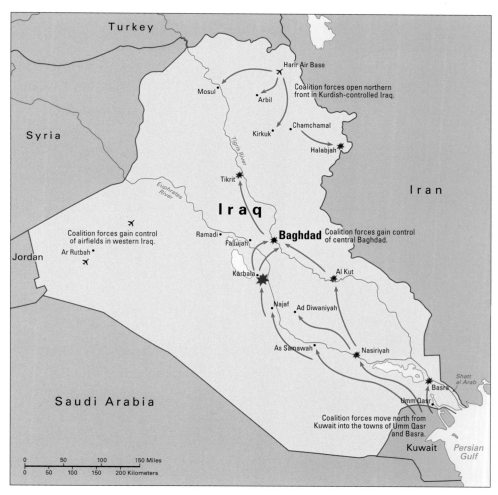

At the beginning of the Iraq War, in 2003, coalition ground forces invaded Iraq from the south, traveling from Kuwait toward Baghdad. Additional troops parachuted into northern Iraq.

The city of Baghdad

Baghdad is Iraq's capital and one of the Middle East's largest cities. Today the city has about 5 million people. It is Iraq's chief center of culture, manufacturing, trade, and transportation. The city lies on both banks of the Tigris River, about 335 miles (539 kilometers) northwest of the Persian Gulf.

Baghdad became an important city during the A.D. 700's. Through the centuries, it has survived repeated damage by wars, fires, and floods. The city covers about 254 square miles (657 square kilometers) on a fertile plain that is Iraq's agricultural heartland. Central Baghdad has two main districts—Karkh, on the west bank of the Tigris, and Rusafah, on the east bank. Parts of Karkh and Rusafah have narrow streets and colorful bazaars. Central Baghdad also has modern banks, department stores, and hotels. Industrial and residential districts extend in all directions from central Baghdad. Kadhamain, an Islamic holy city, in located in Baghdad.

Most of the people of Baghdad are Muslim Arabs. Jews, Christian Arabs, and Muslim Iranians and Kurds make up minority groups in the city. Arabic is the chief language, but most of the Iranians and Kurds also speak their own language.

People have lived in what is now the Baghdad area since about 4000 B.C. This area formed part of ancient Babylonia. From the 500's B.C. to the A.D. 600's, Persians, Greeks, and then Romans controlled the area. An Islamic dynasty, the Abbasids, gained control of the region in 750. In 762, Abu Jafar al-Mansur, an Abbasid *caliph* (ruler), began building Baghdad as the site for the new capital of the Arab Muslim empire. At that time, the empire extended from western North Africa to western China. By 800, Baghdad

Baghdad, Iraq's capital and largest city, has wide boulevards and modern buildings in its central area, shown here. Other areas have dusty streets and colorful bazaars. Baghdad came under heavy bombardment during the Persian Gulf War of 1991 and the Iraq War.

had nearly a million people and was a world center of education and Islamic culture. From the 1000's to the 1200's, Baghdad gradually lost power and wealth. In 1258, Mongols from Central Asia ended the empire and destroyed Baghdad. Mongols, Persians, or Turks controlled Baghdad until about 1535, when it became part of the Ottoman Empire. By the late 1700's, only about 15,000 people lived there. In the 1800's, the Ottoman government restored the city, and by 1900, the population of Baghdad was nearly 100,000.

During World War I (1914-1918), British troops captured what is now Iraq from the Ottoman Empire. In 1932, Iraq became an independent nation with Baghdad as its capital.

Baghdad suffered heavy bombing by allied forces during the Persian Gulf War of 1991 and the Iraq War. U.S.-led forces bombed military targets in the city, and militants and suicide bombers carried out attacks on coalition and civilian targets. Also, sectarian violence has killed thousands of people in Baghdad.

By late 2003, U.S. President George W. Bush had begun to face significant criticism about the Iraq War. In this photograph, protesters from across the United States march past the White House in Washington, D.C., in October 2003.

to rebuild Iraq. In May 2003, the U.N. Security Council had granted the United States and the United Kingdom broad powers to rule Iraq until a new government could be formed.

Some Iraqis continued to oppose the presence of the U.S.-led forces. U.S. forces became the target of guerrilla-style attacks. The attackers, who included suicide bombers, also targeted Iraqis and international organizations that could be seen as cooperating with U.S. forces.

By late 2003, Bush had begun to face significant criticism about the war. United States casualties mounted. No weapons of mass destruction had been found in Iraq. Some critics charged that, before the invasion of Iraq, Bush had used misleading or inaccurate information on Iraq's weapons programs to justify the war. In February 2004, Bush announced the formation of a commission to examine American intelligence-gathering operations.

In May 2004, the Bush administration began investigating reports that U.S. soldiers had abused Iraqi prisoners of war. Photographs taken at Abu Ghraib (*AH boo GREHB*), a U.S.-run prison in Iraq, supported the claims. The photos showed U.S. soldiers threatening, beating, and humiliating Iraqi prisoners. The photos led to criminal charges against several U.S. soldiers.

In March 2005, the commission formed to examine American intelligence-gathering operations issued its report. The commission was to find out why apparently inaccurate information had been provided to

Abu Ghraib prison is a facility near Baghdad, in Iraq. U.S. forces detained prisoners of war, including suspected terrorists, at the prison during the first three years of the Iraq War. In this photograph, U.S. soldiers stand guard as prisoners are released in 2006.

Abu Ghraib prison

Abu Ghraib prison is near Baghdad, in Iraq. United States forces detained prisoners of war, including suspected terrorists, at the prison during the first three years of the Iraq War. Abu Ghraib became the subject of international controversy in 2004 when photographs were released showing U.S. soldiers abusing Iraqi prisoners at the facility.

In the mid-1960's, British contractors began the construction of Abu Ghraib about 20 miles (32 kilometers) west of central Baghdad. The 280-acre (113-hectare) prison opened in 1970.

The prison gained a reputation for brutality after Saddam Hussein became president of Iraq in 1979. Reports indicated that thousands of political prisoners were tortured and executed at the prison, primarily during the Iran-Iraq War (1980-1988). Many of those killed were Shī`ite Muslims, Kurds, or Iraqis of Iranian origin. Investigators later found the sites of several mass graves within or near the prison grounds.

In 2002, U.S. authorities, arguing that Hussein had been concealing illegal weapons programs, began building a case for the invasion of Iraq. On Oct. 20, 2002, Hussein declared an *amnesty* (forgiveness for past crimes) for the prisoners inside Abu Ghraib. Some reports claimed that as many as 13,000 inmates were freed.

American authorities began holding prisoners of war and other "high value" detainees at Abu Ghraib in mid-2003. Officers of the U.S. Army's 800th Military Police Brigade were among the authorities that oversaw the prison.

In January 2004, the military began an investigation of reports of prisoner abuse at Abu Ghraib. On April 28, news reports revealed photographs showing American guards threatening, beating, and sexually humiliating prisoners there. The photos had been taken in late 2003. The Bush administration soon began an investigation into guards' conduct at the prison. The investigation led to criminal charges against 11 soldiers, including military police and members of a military intelligence unit that interrogated prisoners. Nine of the soldiers received prison sentences. Private First Class Lynndie R. England, who featured prominently in the photographs, was sentenced in September 2005 to three years in a military prison. The alleged ringleader of the abuses, Corporal Charles A. Graner, Jr., received a 10-year sentence in January 2005.

The scandal sparked international outrage and condemnation, particularly from Muslims and human rights groups. Public opinion polls suggested that the scandal had damaged the international reputation of the United States and turned many Americans against the war. The United States closed the prison in 2006 and transferred some 4,500 of its prisoners to detention centers elsewhere in Iraq. Iraqi authorities then assumed control of the facility. Iraqi authorities upgraded the prison, now called Baghdad Central Prison, before reopening it in 2009.

In July 2013, the Islamic State attacked the prison and freed more than 500 prisoners. The Iraqi government temporarily shut down the prison in April 2014. Authorities said they feared that the prison could become overrun by ISIS militants. About 2,400 prisoners there were transferred to other prisons.

the president about Iraq's weapons of mass destruction. The commission's report criticized the nation's intelligence agencies. The commission made recommendations for improving intelligence gathering and analysis. Bush endorsed the recommendations and began acting upon them. In June, Bush created a National Security Service within the Federal Bureau of Investigation (FBI). The National Security Service would specialize in intelligence and other national security matters.

The U.S.-led coalition forces remained in Iraq to provide security during Iraq's transition to a constitutional government. In January 2005, Iraqi voters elected a transitional National Assembly. The Assembly oversaw the preparation of a new constitution. In October, Iraqis approved the constitution in a nationwide *referendum* (direct vote). In December, Iraqi voters elected a new legislature. Members of the new Council of Representatives took office in March 2006. The council approved a prime minister and Council of Ministers in May.

Attacks by militant groups continued against coalition forces and Iraqi police and civilians. In a nationally televised speech in January 2007, Bush called for more than 20,000 additional U.S. troops to be sent to Iraq. He said the soldiers were needed to help the Iraqi government gain control of Baghdad and Al Anbar province, west of Baghdad. Those two areas had suffered some of Iraq's most intense conflict. Many Democrats and some Republicans in Congress said Bush's plan would put a strain on the military. They called for the president to bring the troops home.

On May 1, 2007, Bush vetoed a war-funding bill passed by the Democratic-led Congress. The veto was the second of his presidency. He objected to the bill's requirement that he begin withdrawing troops from Iraq later in the year. He called the bill a timetable for failure. A deadline for withdrawal, he said, would take power from U.S. military

David Petraeus

Army General David Petraeus (*puh TRAY uhs*) (1952-   ) served as the commanding general of U.S. and multinational forces in both Iraq and Afghanistan. He was responsible for the development of the Army and Marine Corps *counterinsurgency* doctrine that was later deployed in Iraq and Afghanistan. In 2007, he was promoted to the rank of four-star general. He took command of the Multi-National Force-Iraq. Petraeus was the architect of the so-called *troop surge* strategy in 2007, when the United States sent 30,000 more troops to help the Iraqi government establish security throughout the country. That strategy was credited with reducing violence in Iraq.

Petraeus's success in Iraq earned him command of the U.S. Central Command and responsibility for the wars in Iraq and Afghanistan. In July 2010, he took command of U.S. forces in Afghanistan and of the NATO International Security Assistance Forces in Afghanistan. He retired from the Army in August 2011.

U.S. President George W. Bush makes a statement to reporters on May 10, 2007, about the war in Iraq after his meeting with senior national defense leaders at the Pentagon. On May 1, Bush vetoed a war-funding bill passed by the Democratic-led Congress.

leaders. It would further destabilize Iraq and the Middle East. Congress sent Bush the bill on May 1. It was the fourth anniversary of the 2003 date on which Bush said major military operations in Iraq had ended. Democratic leaders said the American people expected Congress to end U.S. involvement in Iraq. Public opinion polls at the time said most Americans favored a withdrawal schedule. Polls also said most Americans wanted the troops sufficiently funded even without a timetable.

By June 15, 2007, all of the additional troops—about 30,000—that Bush had requested had arrived in Iraq. The so-called "surge" in troop levels was intended to help the Iraqi government establish long-term security throughout the country.

In March 2008, Bush marked the fifth anniversary of the start of the Iraq War. Political instability continued in Iraq. But administration officials said that casualties for coalition troops, Iraqi security forces, and Iraqi civilians had decreased from levels of the prior year. Later that month, officials reported that 4,000 members of the U.S. military had died since the war started in 2003. According to news reports at the time, about 90,000 Iraqi civilians had been killed during the conflicts.

U.S. troops say goodbye to their loved ones at Dallas Fort Worth Airport in Dallas, Texas, in August 2007, before departing for operations overseas in the Iraq War.

Tommy Franks

Tommy Ray Franks (1945-   ), a United States Army general, headed the American-led forces during the initial combat phase of the Iraq War. Franks was commander in chief of the U.S. Central Command from 2000 to mid-2003. In that post, he was responsible for overseeing U.S. military operations in 25 countries of Africa, Asia, and the Middle East, including Iraq. In 2001, he commanded the forces of the United States and its allies in Afghanistan, where the allied forces helped overthrow the country's Taliban leaders.

Franks was born on June 17, 1945, in Wynnewood, Oklahoma. He grew up in Midland, Texas, where his family moved when he was a boy. Franks earned a bachelor's degree in business administration from the University of Texas at Arlington in 1971 and a master's degree in public administration from Shippensburg University in 1985.

Franks's military career began in 1965 when he joined the U.S. Army. He was commissioned a second lieutenant in 1967 after completing artillery officer candidate school at Fort Sill, Oklahoma. He then served for a year in Vietnam during the Vietnam War (1957-1975) and was wounded three times.

Franks moved up through Army ranks as he held posts in West Germany and at the Pentagon. During the Persian Gulf War of 1991, he was an assistant division commander of the First Cavalry Division. He headed the Second Infantry Division in South Korea

United States Army General Tommy Franks, using a map of
Iraq, reports on the progress of U.S.-led military operations
against Iraq in 2003, during the Iraq War.

from 1995 to 1997. From 1997 to 2000, he was the commander of
the Third U.S. Army.

   In 2000, Franks became commander in chief of the U.S. Central
Command and received the rank of general. He retired from the
post and from the U.S. Army in July 2003. His autobiography,
American Soldier, was published in 2004. Also in 2004, Franks was
awarded the Presidential Medal of Freedom.

Antiwar protesters participate in a march in 2003 in Augusta, Maine. Several hundred people turned out to show their opposition to the war in Iraq. Many critics charged that U.S. President George W. Bush and British Prime Minister Tony Blair used misleading, inaccurate, or false information to justify the war.

Opposition to the war

Some people, including former UN Secretary-General Kofi Annan, argued that the invasion of Iraq violated international law. Some feared that the war, and disagreements over its timing and justification, weakened the UN and other international institutions.

Bush and British Prime Minister Tony Blair faced significant criticism over the conflict. Many critics charged that Bush and Blair used misleading, inaccurate, or false information to justify the war. Before the war, Bush and Blair said that Iraq possessed weapons of mass destruction. However, after the Hussein regime was overthrown, coalition inspectors failed to find any such weapons in Iraq. Investigators concluded that U.S. and British intelligence agencies provided inaccurate estimates of Iraq's weapons capabilities before the war.

Bush and Blair also claimed that there were links between Iraq and al-Qa`ida. The Hussein regime did support terrorist groups fighting the governments of Turkey and Iran, as well as Palestinian terrorist groups. In addition, some contacts apparently occurred between Iraqi officials and Qa`ida representatives. However, there is no evidence that a working relationship ever developed between Iraq and al-Qa`ida.

Supporters of the war argued that it was necessary to prevent Iraq from developing weapons of mass destruction and supplying them to terrorist groups. They also argued that Hussein needed to be removed from power because he was a brutal dictator. Hussein had authorized the extermination of hundreds of thousands of his own people, and he had shown disregard for the fundamental principles of international relations.

By 2004, the Bush administration had made democracy in Iraq a central goal of the war. It argued that if Iraq successfully developed a democratic government, democracy would then spread throughout the Middle East. But as the conflict dragged on, worldwide public opinion had increasingly come to oppose the continuing U.S. military presence in Iraq.

Opposition to the war made it a major issue in the 2008 U.S. presidential election. Many argued that the war was a mistake because of the determination that Iraq had no weapons of mass destruction. This became a factor in the decision to end combat operations. Consternation about the war continued as stability in Iraq remained an issue and the radical Sunni group the Islamic State (often referred to by the initials ISIS or ISIL) became a threat.

Sunni militants bombed the al-Askari shrine on Feb. 22, 2006. The bombing led to violence between Sunni and Shī`ite Muslims and made it more difficult for U.S.-led forces to provide security for Iraqis. The shrine, in Samarra, 60 miles (95 kilometers) north of Baghdad, is one of the holiest sites to Shī`ite Muslims. In this 2011 photograph, scaffolding surrounds the dome and minaret.

Rebuilding in Iraq

While developing a new Iraqi government, the U.S.-led coalition addressed the task of building security forces and increasing safety in all parts of the country, which had become destabilized after major combat. Sectarian violence, terrorism, and falling public opinion complicated nation-building operations.

During most of the period from 2003 to 2009, U.S. troops provided security in northern and western Iraq; British troops provided security in much of southern Iraq; and a Polish-led international force had security duties in an area of central Iraq south of Baghdad. Iraqi troops became increasingly involved in security operations, especially after June 2004. Nearly 40 countries sent peacekeeping forces to serve in Iraq. Besides the United States, participating countries included Albania, Armenia, Australia, Azerbaijan, Bosnia-Herzegovina, Bulgaria, the Czech Republic, Denmark, the Dominican Republic, El Salvador, Estonia, Fiji, Georgia, Honduras, Hungary, Italy, Japan, Kazakhstan, Latvia, Lithuania, Macedonia, Moldova, Mongolia, the Netherlands, New Zealand, Nicaragua, Norway, the Philippines, Poland, Portugal, Romania, Slovakia, South Korea, Spain, Thailand, Tonga, Ukraine, and the United Kingdom.

Many Iraqis celebrated the fall of Hussein's government. However, many also opposed the presence of U.S. and other foreign forces in Iraq. On numerous occasions, the opposition became violent.

After Bush declared the end of major combat operations in May 2003, many guerrilla attacks, bombings, and other violent acts continued in Iraq. Militants from both the Sunni Muslim and Shī`ite Muslim populations in Iraq carried out attacks and called for the withdrawal of foreign soldiers and civilians. Before 2006, most of the militants were Sunnis who opposed Iraq's new government, which was dominated by Shī`ites and backed by the United States. Some of the attackers were believed to be loyal to Hussein.

Muslim militants from other countries were thought to have been involved in many attacks in Iraq. Some of the militants were believed to have connections to al-Qa`ida. The main group of militants with Qa`ida ties was led by Abu Musab al-Zarqawi, a Jordanian, until his death in June 2006. This group is sometimes called by its original name, Tawhid and Jihad. It has also been called al-Qa`ida in Iraq, al-Qa`ida Organization of Holy War in Iraq, and other names that indicate its Qa`ida connections.

The attacks targeted coalition troops, Iraqi security forces, and Iraqi and foreign civilians. Some of the attacks struck against religious sites, especially Shī`ite ones. Several Iraqis in key leadership positions were assassinated. Bombing targets included police and civil defense stations, government buildings, military facilities, oil pipelines, mosques, and churches. High-profile targets included the Jordanian embassy in Baghdad; the UN headquarters in Baghdad; the Imam Ali Mosque in Najaf, a major holy site for Shī`ites; the headquarters of the Red Cross in Baghdad; Kurdish political party offices in Arbil; and sites in Baghdad and Karbala where Shī`ites gather each year for the religious festival of Ashura.

Hundreds of Iraqi and foreign civilians were kidnapped in Iraq. Many of the kidnappings were for ransom, but others were for political reasons. For example, some militants kidnapped foreign civilians to persuade their home countries to withdraw troops from, or cease business activities in, Iraq. Kidnappers murdered some of the civilians.

In 2004, frequent clashes between Sunni militants and U.S.-led forces began in central Iraq. The city of Fallujah (*fah LOO juh*), west of Baghdad, was the site of much of the fighting. The violence killed thousands

Improvised explosive devices

With the fall of the Iraqi government, militants gained access to stockpiles of military explosives. They used these as the main charges in improvised explosive devices (IED's), which were homemade. Such explosives varied by region. Many of these explosives employed chemicals used in local agriculture. Terrorists and guerrilla fighters, lacking military-grade weapons, often make and use IED's. They plant the explosives as booby traps along roads—where they may be referred to as *roadside bombs*—or in buildings. Militants and guerrilla fighters often attach IED's to vehicles.

An IED consists of two main parts. They are an *initiating system* and a *main charge.* The initiating system usually contains a small amount of a sensitive *primary explosive.* Initiating systems can be triggered in various ways, such as with trip wires, pressure plates, and electronic devices. When the initiating system's primary explosive detonates, it creates a shock wave. This shock wave, in turn, sets off the main charge, also called the *secondary explosive.* This charge provides most of the weapon's explosive energy and potential to do serious damage and harm. Some IED's require a *booster* that helps set off the main charge by amplifying the primary explosive's shock wave.

A remote-control bomb-defusing robot operated by a U.S. Army bomb squad pulls the wire of a suspected improvised explosive device (IED) in Samarra, Iraq in 2004.

of people, including soldiers, militants, and civilians. In mid-2004, Sunni militants gained control of some parts of central Iraq, including the cities of Fallujah, Ramadi (*ruh MAH dee*), and Samarra (*suh MAHR uh*). In October 2004, U.S. and Iraqi forces regained control of Samarra. In November, after several weeks of U.S. air strikes on Fallujah, U.S. and Iraqi forces began a major ground assault on the city. They seized control of most of Fallujah within a few days. The air and ground attacks destroyed hundreds of buildings and did much damage to the city's power lines and water and sewer pipes.

Also in 2004, much fighting occurred between U.S.-led forces and militants loyal to the radical Shī`ite cleric Muqtada (also spelled Moqtada) al-Sadr (*mook TAH duh ehl SAH dur*), an outspoken critic of the occupation. This fighting took place mainly in Najaf and in a Baghdad community known as Sadr City. The uprising, one of several Al-Sadr led against the coalition, came after coalition authorities banned a radical newspaper that al-Sadr had established. The authorities claimed that he used the paper to stir anti-U.S. sentiments and to incite violence. Al-Sadr later signed a truce with the Iraqi government, which was facilitated by Iraq's most influential Shī`ite cleric, Grand Ayatollah (*ah yuh TOHL uh*) Ali al-Sistani (*AH lee ahl sihs TAH nee*), and partially disarmed his militia.

Al-Sistani's role in promoting peace and voting participation during the occupation was important to the recovery of Iraq and symbolized how politically adept he had been throughout his life.

A new government in Iraq

While the U.S.-led coalition fought to stabilize Iraq and develop Iraqi security forces, Iraqi citizens elected its new government. The coalition countries, led by the United States, established the Coalition Provisional

A U.S. Army Stryker armored vehicle passes an Iraqi woman as she leaves Fallujah, Iraq, in April 2004. The city, west of Baghdad, was the site of frequent clashes between Sunni militants and U.S.-led forces that year. The violence killed thousands of people, including soldiers, militants, and civilians.

In mid-2004, Sunni militants gained control of some
parts of central Iraq, including the city of Ramadi.
In this photograph, U.S. Marines position themselves
along the roads to block traffic during a cordon and
search in the city. The Marines were searching the
area for insurgents and weapons caches.

Authority (CPA) as a temporary government for Iraq. Looting broke out
in several cities, and coalition troops and CPA officials then focused on
restoring order and overseeing the creation of a new Iraqi-controlled
government. On June 28, 2004, the CPA was dissolved, and an interim
government made up of Iraqis took its place.

In January 2005, Iraqi voters elected a transitional National Assembly

for Iraq to replace the interim government. Before the election, Sunni militants had threatened to disrupt the election with violence. Nevertheless, nearly 60 percent of all eligible voters went to the polls. Most of the voters were Shī`ite Arabs and Kurds, and a Shī`ite religious alliance won a majority of seats in the Assembly. A large number of Iraq's Sunni Arabs *boycotted* (refused to participate in) the election. Many objected

Ali al-Sistani

Ali al-Sistani (*AH lee ahl sihs TAH nee*) (1930-   ) was born into a prominent family of Shī`ite scholars on Aug. 4, 1930, in Meshed, Iran. He began studying religion at an early age. In 1949, he continued his education in the city of Qom, Iran, a center of Shī`ite learning. A few years later, he moved to the Shī`ite holy city of Najaf, Iraq. In 1960, al-Sistani became a *mujtahid,* or Shī`ite scholar. In 1992, he was named a Grand Ayatollah. This is the highest religious position that can be held by a Shī`ite Muslim.

Al-Sistani believes that Shī`ite religious leaders should remain independent from politics. This belief, called *quietism,* has a long history in Shī`ism, but it is not shared by all Shī`ite religious leaders. Al-Sistani's rejection of politics allowed him to work during the regime of Saddam Hussein, from 1979 to 2003, when many Shī`ite leaders were persecuted.

Since 2003, when the United States led an invasion of Iraq and brought down the Hussein government, al-Sistani has advocated free elections and self-determination for the Iraqi people. At the same time, he has stressed the need for Shī`ite scholars to provide guidance on religious matters. Throughout the Iraq War, al-Sistani has encouraged peaceful public demonstrations, called on the Iraqi people to vote, and helped resolve conflicts between rival factions.

to the *proportional representation* system introduced in the Assembly under the interim constitution. Such representation awards a political party a percentage of assembly seats in proportion to its share of the total votes cast. Some Sunnis also stayed away from the polls for fear that they would be attacked.

In April 2005, Ibrahim al-Jafari, a Shī`ite, was named interim prime minister of Iraq. Jafari was part of the United Iraqi Alliance (UIA), the political group that won the National Assembly election. The National Assembly oversaw the preparation of a new constitution for Iraq. In October, Iraqis approved the constitution in a nationwide *referendum* (direct vote).

In December 2005, Iraqis elected a permanent Council of Representatives to replace the National Assembly. The Council of Representatives took office in March 2006. The UIA received the most seats and nominated Jafari as prime minister. However, the other parties in the Assembly did not accept his nomination. He withdrew his candidacy in April 2006. The UIA then nominated Nouri Kamel al-Maliki (*NOOR ee kah MIHL al MAL ih kee*) (1950-   ), a Shī`ite, as prime minister, and the council approved his nomination. He became prime minister in May. The council also elected Jalal Talabani (*juh LAHL tah lah BAH nee*) (1933-   ), a Kurd who had served as interim president, to a four-year term as president.

In March 2010 elections, a Maliki-led coalition narrowly lost to a group led by former prime minister Iyad Allawi. After months of negotiations, a new government was formed in November with Maliki remaining as prime minister.

In 2011, antigovernment protests erupted in several Iraqi cities. Protesters called for improved government services and an end to official corruption. In 2013, increasing sectarian violence in Iraq—mainly

In January 2005, Iraqi voters elected a transitional National Assembly. The Assembly oversaw the preparation of a new constitution. In October, Iraqis approved the constitution in a nationwide *referendum* (direct vote). In this photograph, an Iraqi Sunni woman votes in the October referendum.

between Sunnis and Shī`ites—killed thousands of people. Thousands more died in 2014 as attacks by the Islamic State in Iraq and Syria (ISIS) (later simply the Islamic State) pushed Iraq to the brink of civil war.

In August, Iraq's newly elected president, Kurdish politician Fuad Masum (*foo AHD mah SUHM*) (1938-   ), named Haider al-Abadi (*HY duhr al uh BAH dee*) (1952-   ), a Shī`ite, to replace Maliki as prime minister. That same month, a large coalition of nations, including the United States, France, the United Kingdom, and Saudi Arabia, united to confront the Islamic State threat. Coalition air strikes against Islamic State targets in northern Iraq intensified through the year and continued through 2015, 2016, and into 2017. A number of U.S., Canadian, and other coalition troops supported Iraqi troops and Kurdish security forces battling the extremists on the ground.

The number of attacks in Iraq dropped, but some violence continued. United States combat operations in Iraq formally ended on Aug. 31, 2010. Some U.S. troops remained in Iraq until late 2011 to fight terrorism and perform other duties.

Consequences of the war

A total of 172 coalition soldiers—139 Americans and 33 Britons—died during what Bush called the major combat phase of the war in March and April 2003. From May 1, 2003, until the war's official end on Dec. 15, 2011, an additional 4,631 coalition soldiers, mostly Americans, died in Iraq. More than 32,000 coalition soldiers were wounded. There are no official estimates of how many Iraqis died in the war. Most observers believe that tens of thousands of Iraqis, mostly civilians, died. Some observers believe there were several hundred thousand Iraqi deaths. Numerous foreign civilians, including journalists, business people, and aid workers, were also killed.

In 2011, antigovernment protests erupted in several Iraqi cities. Protesters called for improved government services and an end to official corruption. In this photograph, Iraqis demonstrate at Tahrir Square in Baghdad in March of that year.

Mosul

Mosul (*moh SOOL*), also called al-Mawsil, is one of Iraq's largest cities and an important commercial center. About 1,700,000 people live in the city. Mosul lies on the west bank of the Tigris River in northern Iraq.

Partly because of its location, Mosul has long been an important trading center. The ruins of the ancient city of Nineveh lie just across the Tigris River from Mosul. Mosul was once known for producing high-quality cotton goods. *Muslin,* a fine cotton cloth, took its name from the city.

Since the 1930's, oil from the Mosul region has given the area new importance in world markets. Mosul's population—a mixture of Arabs, Kurds, and Turkomans, among others—reflects the historical role the region has played as a frontier. Most of the city's people are Muslims.

The city has been vulnerable to conflicts of the past 26 years. Mosul suffered damage from bombing during the Persian Gulf War of 1991. During the 1990's and early 2000's, the city suffered occasional Kurdish uprisings and frequent attacks by United States and British warplanes on Iraqi military targets. Mosul again became a scene of fighting and bombing during the Iraq War.

In June 2014, a radical extremist group known as the Islamic State took control of Mosul. The group had been previously known as the Islamic State in Iraq and Syria (ISIS). The group killed thousands of the city's citizens and forced others into slavery. In February 2015, Islamic State militants burned the Mosul Library, destroying thousands of ancient manuscripts.

In 2014, the Islamic State destroyed a revered structure in Mosul purported to be the tomb of the Biblical prophet Jonah.

They also destroyed ancient statues at Mosul's Nirgal Gate and artifacts at the Mosul Museum.

From October 2016 to July 2017, Mosul was heavily damaged as Iraqi and Kurdish troops battled Islamic State militants for control of the city. During the fighting, Islamic State militants destroyed Mosul's historic Grand Mosque of al-Nuri. In July 2017, Iraq's government declared that it had defeated the Islamic State for control of Mosul.

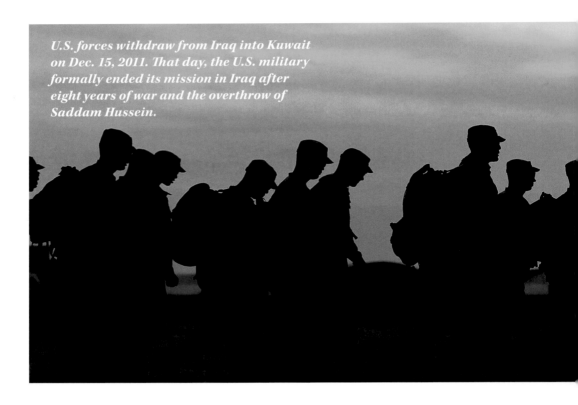

U.S. forces withdraw from Iraq into Kuwait on Dec. 15, 2011. That day, the U.S. military formally ended its mission in Iraq after eight years of war and the overthrow of Saddam Hussein.

The war caused extensive damage to Iraq's utilities, transportation systems, and industries. In addition, looting was a major problem during the early stages of the war, as mobs of Iraqis entered palaces, museums, and other buildings and carried away items from inside.

World opinion was sharply divided over the war and the occupation of Iraq by coalition forces. Before the war began, most Americans supported the invasion of Iraq. But the invasion and the occupation also received much criticism, both inside and outside the United States. Before the war began, antiwar protesters held numerous demonstrations in the United States and in many other countries. Additional demonstrations took place throughout the period of the invasion and occupation.

Many opponents of the war argued that it inspired anger and resent-

ment among Arabs and Muslims toward the United States and its allies. Many people believed such hostility caused an increase in terrorist violence against U.S. targets.

Another important consequence of the Iraq War was the development of the Islamic State. The Sunni fundamentalist group, based in Iraq and Syria, emerged from the chaos of the Iraq War and the Syrian Civil War, which began in 2011. By 2014, the group had established control over parts of Iraq and Syria. Thousands died in attacks.

The Islamic State faces serious opposition from the Iraqi and Syrian militaries, Shi`ite militias, and other militant groups, as well as from Kurdish forces in northern Iraq and Syria. In addition, a large group of nations, including the United States, Russia, and Turkey, has confronted

Islamic State

Islamic State is the name used by a radical militant Islamic group based in Iraq and Syria. The group was formerly associated with the terrorist organization al-Qa`ida. The Islamic State has roots in two main conflicts: the Iraq War and the Syrian Civil War that began in 2011. Other names for the group have included the Islamic State in Iraq and Syria (ISIS) and the Islamic State in Iraq and the Levant (ISIL). The term *Levant* refers to countries around the eastern Mediterranean Sea. The acronym *DAESH,* based on the group's full Arabic name (al-Dawla al-Islamiya fi al-Iraq wa al-Sham), is also used.

The Islamic State is a Sunni Muslim group known for its ruthless violence and severe interpretation of the Sharī`ah, the legal and moral code of Islam. Led by Iraqi militant Abu Bakr al-Baghdadi (*AH boo BAH kuhr al bahg DAH dee*), the Islamic State has killed thousands of civilians, military personnel, and rival militants. The group specifically targets rival Shī`ite Muslims, Christians, and anyone else it deems an "enemy of Islam." Most Islamic State fighters are Iraqi or Syrian, though the group also includes other Muslims from around the world.

In 2003, a U.S.-led coalition invaded Iraq and deposed Iraqi leader Saddam Hussein. The United States then helped install a government dominated by Shī`ites, the majority Muslim group in Iraq. Several Sunni militant groups emerged to oppose the new Iraqi government as well as the U.S. occupation. Among these groups was al-Qa`ida in Iraq, which would develop into the Islamic State of Iraq (ISI). Beginning in 2006, ISIS repeatedly attacked military and civilian targets in Iraq.

In 2011, a bitter civil war erupted in neighboring Syria. In 2013, some Sunni rebel groups in Syria joined with ISI, which renamed

A masked gunman waves an Islamic State flag in the northern Iraqi city of Mosul in June 2014. Extremist Islamic State fighters killed thousands of the city's citizens and destroyed numerous historic structures.

itself ISIS. ISIS grew quickly into a potent military organization, fighting Syrian government troops as well as competing rebel groups. Fighting between ISIS and al-Qa`ida's Syrian branch, the al-Nusra (*al NOOS ruh*) Front, caused a sharp break between the groups in early 2014. Al-Qa`ida, known for its own brutality, also wished to separate itself from increasingly vicious ISIS massacres and mass executions.

By mid-2014, ISIS had established control over large parts of Iraq and Syria. In June, the group changed its name to the Islamic State, claiming to have established a *caliphate*. A caliphate is a government ruled by a caliph, a leader with political and religious authority recognized by Muslims as a successor of the Prophet Muhammad. Abu Bakr al-Baghdadi proclaimed himself Caliph Ibrahim.

In 2017, the Islamic State lost much of its conquered territory, including its main bases in Mosul, Iraq, and Raqqa, Syria.

the Islamic State threat in both Iraq and Syria. Since August 2014, combined airstrikes have targeted Islamic State positions, and a limited number of ground forces have also engaged the terror group.

Since early 2015, Islamic State terrorists have made numerous attacks on civilians in Iraq and Syria, with highly publicized attacks also taking place in Belgium, Egypt, France, Libya, Tunisia, Turkey, the United Kingdom, Yemen, and other nations.

In 2017, the Islamic State lost much of its conquered territory, including its main bases in Mosul, Iraq, and Raqqa, Syria.

Men walk past destroyed buildings in Mosul, Iraq's second largest city. From October 2016 to July 2017, Mosul was heavily damaged as Iraqi and Kurdish troops battled Islamic State militants for control of the city.

About 200 Shī`ite volunteers from Tal Afar, in northern Iraq, attend a combat training session at a military camp in the Shī`ite shrine city of Karbala in central Iraq in 2014. The volunteers were joining the fight against jihadists of the Islamic State.

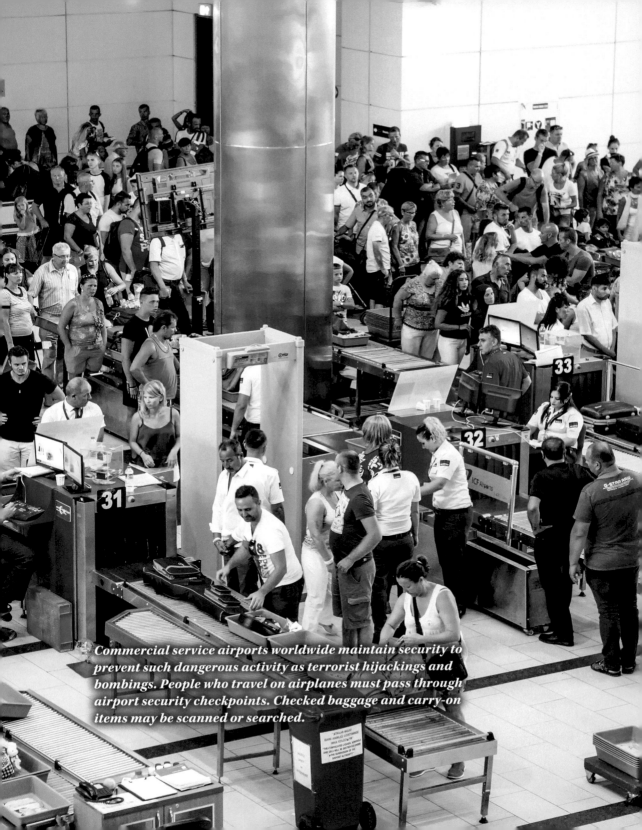

Commercial service airports worldwide maintain security to prevent such dangerous activity as terrorist hijackings and bombings. People who travel on airplanes must pass through airport security checkpoints. Checked baggage and carry-on items may be scanned or searched.

CHAPTER FOUR

Security and civil rights in times of crisis

Following the terrorist attacks of Sept. 11, 2001, on the World Trade Center in New York City and the Pentagon Building near Washington, D. C., President George W. Bush addressed Congress and a grieving nation. He described the challenges facing the United States:

"Tonight we are a country awakened to danger and called to defend freedom. Our grief has turned to anger, and anger to resolution.... I know there are struggles ahead and dangers to face. But this country will define our times, not be defined by them."

The challenges of the war against terrorism are many. One of the most significant is the need to provide effective national security while respecting the rights of citizens of and visitors to the United States. The government's ability to prevent terrorist attacks depends largely on its ability to intercept communication to and from terrorist suspects, to search individuals for weapons and dangerous materials, and to investigate and detain suspected terrorists. However, many of these steps require the people in the United States to sacrifice a certain degree of freedom and privacy.

William H. Rehnquist, chief justice of the Supreme Court of the United States, once wrote, "Generally, chief executives in wartime are not very sympathetic to the protection of civil liberties." At various points throughout history, the same has been said of both the United States

Congress and the Supreme Court. Although temporary sacrifices of certain liberties may be necessary to maintain the nation's security, a word of caution comes to us from one of America's founders. Benjamin Franklin, in 1759, wrote that "they that can give up essential liberty to purchase a little temporary safety, deserve neither liberty nor safety."

This chapter explores past and present attempts to find a proper balance between civil rights and national security during times of crisis.

In time of war, the laws are silent

In the more than two centuries since the framing of the U.S. Constitution, the U.S. government has at times operated under the Roman rule of *Inter anna silent leges,* which means, *In time of war, the laws are silent.* In other words, in times of crisis, government policies have often emphasized security at the expense of liberty. But in most cases, such policies have been scaled back or ended once the crisis has passed.

The Alien and Sedition Acts. In 1798, as the United States prepared for an expected war with France, Congress passed a series of laws known as the Alien and Sedition Acts. One of the laws, the Alien Enemies Act, authorized the president to imprison or deport citizens of enemy nations. The Alien Friends Act permitted citizens of friendly nations to be deported if the president considered them dangerous. The Sedition Act was used to fine or imprison people who encouraged resistance to federal laws or who criticized the government. By passing the acts, the Federalist Party, which controlled Congress at the time, hoped to silence their political opponents. But many people objected to the acts, and after the Democratic-Republican Party defeated the Federalists in the election of 1800, the laws were no longer enforced. Still, the precedent for limiting rights during times of crisis had been established.

During the American Civil War (1861-1865), President Abraham

FIFTH CONGRESS OF THE UNITED STATES:

At the Second Session.

Begun and held at the city of *Philadelphia*, in the state of PENNSYLVANIA. on *Monday*, the thirteenth of *November*, one thousand seven hundred and ninety-seven.

An **ACT** concerning aliens.

The Alien Friends Act, shown here, permitted the president of the United States to deport citizens of friendly nations that were considered dangerous. The act was passed by Congress in 1798 as one of four laws called the Alien and Sedition Acts. These laws also made it a crime for anyone to criticize the president or Congress. All four laws were later repealed, amended, or let expire.

Lincoln authorized the establishment of martial law—that is, a temporary, emergency form of government under military rule—in parts of the North.

Lincoln also suspended the right known as *habeas corpus* in many cases involving Southern sympathizers. Habeas corpus guarantees a person under arrest a chance to be heard in court. The Supreme Court later ruled that the suspension of habeas corpus was unconstitutional.

Also during the Civil War, the Union Army used military commissions to try people accused of creating civil disorder that aided the Confederacy. The government also used a military commission to try several people believed to have been involved in Lincoln's assassination. One year after the Civil War ended, the Supreme Court ruled that trials of civilians by military courts were not constitutional if civilian courts were open and operating at the time.

During the Vietnam War (1957-1975), protests against the war and the military draft were frequent, passionate, and sometimes violent. The government responded by using law enforcement and national guard troops to contain the protests. In addition, government agencies, including the Federal Bureau of Investigation (FBI), began keeping track of protest organizers and attendees. In some cases, the government tapped people's telephones, sometimes without a warrant. Despite these abuses, a growing number of Americans exercised their right to protest. The protests eventually influenced government policy and helped lead to the U.S. withdrawal from the conflict.

Security efforts in the war against terrorism

After the events of September 11, the Bush administration took a number of steps aimed at bringing terrorists to justice and at preventing future acts of terrorism. But as in past cases, many of the government's policies have required significant limitations of civil rights and have led to heated criticism from civil rights activists.

The U.S.A. Patriot Act, also called the Uniting and Strengthening America by Providing Appropriate Tools Required to Intercept and Obstruct Terrorism Act, was passed in October 2001. The act broadens the definition of terrorists to include anyone who has supported a terrorist group, even if the aid had nothing to do with terrorism. The act also gives law enforcement the power to detain for seven days—or, in some cases, indefinitely—any noncitizen suspected of being a risk to national security. One of the act's most controversial provisions grants

A U.S. Navy inshore security boat patrols the port of Djibouti on the western shore of the Gulf of Aden, where Somali piracy is rampant.

authorities greater freedom to conduct searches, in some cases without giving notice to the subject of the search. Other provisions allow authorities to share secret grand jury information and to obtain information from wiretaps.

Detentions and military trials. The terrorists who carried out the September 11 attacks were all Arabs with ties to al-Qa`ida, the terrorist organization that was headed by Osama bin Laden. Al-Qa`ida had a number of training camps in Afghanistan, and bin Laden himself lived there, supported by Afghanistan's Islamic extremist Taliban regime.

Following the attacks of September 11, the U.S. government detained more than 1,000 individuals indefinitely. The government refused to disclose the identities of those being held in custody.

As part of its investigations, the U.S. government also asked several thousand foreign visitors of Arab descent to appear for interviews with the Justice Department and immigration officials. The purpose of the interview process was to find evidence and information that could be used in the war against terrorism.

In October 2001, a coalition of military forces led by the United States began bombing Afghanistan in an attempt to drive the Taliban from power and to destroy al-Qaʻida operations there. In November 2001, President Bush issued an executive order establishing a system of military tribunals to try noncitizens suspected of terrorism. By using military trials, with military judges and fewer defendants' rights, the president hoped that justice could be made swifter and more secure. In January 2002, the first Taliban and al-Qaʻida detainees from the war in Afghanistan arrived at Camp X-Ray, a prison camp at the U.S. naval base at Guantánamo Bay, Cuba. The detainees were to be subject to questioning and possible trial by military tribunals.

Criticisms. A number of people have questioned some of the steps taken in the war on terrorism. For example, many people have charged that the U.S.A. Patriot Act threatens individuals' privacy and civil rights. The detention of noncitizens for an indefinite period and without releasing their names has led some to raise questions of whether the detainees were being denied "due process of law," as guaranteed by the Fifth Amendment to the U.S. Constitution. Because the requests to foreign visitors in the United States to report for interviews with the Justice Department and immigration officials were directed to people of Arab descent, many groups accused the government of *racial profiling*. Racial profiling involves targeting people for investigation primarily because of racial or ethnic characteristics rather than because there is *probable cause* (good reason for assuming) that the people committed a crime. Many people also criticized the decision to create military tribunals, again partly because of the possible denial of due process, including the right of appeal.

In December 2001, Attorney General John D. Ashcroft responded to critics of administration policies. He stated: "To those ... who scare peace-loving people with phantoms of lost liberty, my message is this: Your tactics only aid terrorists, for they erode our national unity and diminish our resolve." Ashcroft's statement drew harsh criticism from many free-speech advocates.

Determining the proper balance. As the United States and other nations face the challenge of rooting out, combating, and bringing to justice the perpetrators of terrorist violence, governments may make use of sweeping new powers of law enforcement. But as the campaign against terrorism plays out, governments will need to address a number of important questions: What happens when there is no formal declaration of war? For how long will the public continue to accept the personal sacrifices required by government investigations and security procedures? At what point will the crisis be declared over, and for how long will antiterrorist security measures remain in effect? Governments' policies during these times will likely become the benchmarks by which future governments will measure their own policies.

FIND OUT MORE!

Darman, Peter. *Blood, Sweat and Steel: Frontline Accounts from the Gulf, Afghanistan and Iraq.* New Holland Pubs., 2010.

Schwab, Orrin. *The Gulf Wars and the United States: Shaping the Twenty-First Century.* Greenwood, 2009.

Tucker, Spencer C., and Roberts, P. M., eds. *The Encyclopedia of Middle East Wars: the United States in the Persian Gulf, Afghanistan, and Iraq Conflicts.* 5 vols. ABC-CLIO, 2010.

Williams, Brian G. *Afghanistan Declassified: A Guide to America's Longest War.* Univ. of Penn. Pr., 2011.

ACKNOWLEDGMENTS

Cover: © Ethan Miller, Getty Images; © FrozenShutter/ iStockphoto; © Scott Nelson, Getty Images; © Patrick Durand, Sygma/ Getty Images; © Ahmad Al-Rubaye, AFP/Getty Images
4 Tech. Sgt. Efren Lopez, U.S. Air Force
6 © Bernard Estrade, AFP/ Getty Images
9 Public Domain
10 Public Domain
13 © Bettmann/Getty Images
14 © Jacques Pavlovsky, Sygma/Getty Images
16 © Chip Hires, Gamma-Rapho/Getty Images
18 WORLD BOOK map
19 © Three Lions/Getty Images
22-23 © AFP/Getty Images
25 U.S. Army
26 WORLD BOOK map
29 WORLD BOOK map
30-31 National Archives
33 U.S. Army Corps of Engineers
35 WORLD BOOK map
37 © Pascal Guyot, AFP/ Getty Images
39 © Patrick Baz, AFP/Getty Images
40 © Scott Nelson, Getty Images
43 WORLD BOOK map
44 Public Domain
47 © Robert Nickelsberg, Liaison/Getty Images

50 Eric Draper, George W. Bush Presidential Library
51 WORLD BOOK map
52 © Reuters/Landov
53 WORLD BOOK map
54 WORLD BOOK map
55 © Scott Peterson, Getty Images
56 © Universal History Archive/Getty Images
58 WORLD BOOK map
60 © 360b/Shutterstock
62 © Shah Marai, Getty Images
65 Kyle Davis, U.S. Army
66-67 Ashleigh Nushawg (licensed under CC BY 2.0); © Barton Gellman, Getty Images
68-69 Pete Souza, The White House
70-71 Shane T. McCoy, U.S. Navy
72-73 © Shah Marai, Getty Images
74 © Ramzi Haidar, Getty Images
77 © Jon Mills, AP Photo
79 Richard Moore, U.S. Navy
81 WORLD BOOK map
83 © Rasoulali/Shutterstock
84-85 © Luke Frazza, Getty Images; © Ali Jasim, AFP/ Getty Images
89 Central Intelligence Agency
90-91 D. Myles Cullen, U.S. Air Force; © Charles Ommanney, Getty Images
92-93 © Carlo Allegri, Getty Images
94 © Joel Page, AP Photo

96 © Khalid Mohammed, AP Photo
99 Jeremy L. Wood, U.S. Navy
101 © Wathiq Khuzaie, Getty Images
102-103 © AFP/Getty Images
104 Public Domain
106 © Patrick Baz, AFP/Getty Images
108-109 © Getty Images
111 © Lena Ha, Shutterstock
112-113 © Joe Raedle, Getty Images
115 © Reuters/Landov
116-117 © Chris McGrath, Getty Images; © Mohammed Sawaf, AFP/Getty Images
118 © Marius Dobilas, Shutterstock
121 National Archives
123 © Vladimir Melnik, Shutterstock